CONGRATULATIONS, You've Got MS

MEMOIRS OF FAITHFULNESS

MARK ELVERY

WESTBOW
PRESS®
A DIVISION OF THOMAS NELSON
& ZONDERVAN

WestBow Press books may be ordered through booksellers or by contacting:

WestBow Press
A Division of Thomas Nelson & Zondervan
1663 Liberty Drive
Bloomington, IN 47403
www.westbowpress.com
1 (866) 928-1240

congratulations.ms.2018@gmail.com

ISBN: 978-1-9736-4547-4 (sc)
ISBN: 978-1-9736-4549-8 (hc)
ISBN: 978-1-9736-4548-1 (e)

Library of Congress Control Number: 2018913651

Print information available on the last page.

WestBow Press rev. date: 12/21/2018

"…revealed an honest encounter with the living God
that expressed the transformative power of grace…"
Jeff Ireland – *Senior Pastor, Wynnum Baptist
Church, Brisbane, Qld, Australia.*

"…riveting & honest, while constantly seeing & reminding us
how our steps in life have meaning
& have been ordered by a loving Savior…"
Kenny Marks – *Singer, Songwriter,
Recording Artist. Nashville, TN, USA.*

"…not so much a story about the physical and emotional strain
of living with MS but rather it is the story of his journey with
Jesus in the midst of it all…"
Peter Francis – *Principal of Malyon
Theological College. Qld, Australia.*

"…a story of not just the reality of life, but the reality of
God's faithfulness as He rebuilds a broken life…"
Dave Roever – *International speaker, decorated
Vietnam veteran. Fort Worth, TX,, USA.*

"…tells Mark's inspirational story about finding the Lord
in each moment of our lives, including the dark times…"
Linda Nevell – *Editor of the
QB Magazine. Qld, Australia.*

To my beautiful wife and our two sons,
I love you all.
This is Dad!

Contents

Acknowledgments

The first person that I want to thank is my Lord and Savior, Jesus Christ without whom I would not even be around to record this testimony.

My entire family has been instrumental in proving that it was all worth it.

My wife, Adrienne, my best friend, confidante, mother of our children, encourager, and definitely something worth waiting for (I'm just sorry it wasn't sooner!). At times while I was writing this book, you helped me find the words I was looking for and offered advice, smoothing out rough passages as well as helping to fill in vital tidbits of information and facts I had initially overlooked.

My boys, who are having to grow up sooner than many of their peers. I am proud of them and appreciate all that God has blessed me with.

My parents and siblings. Sometimes God uses moments of contention with those who are closest to us to prepare us for future battles and struggles that we will one day face. We have had some of these times, but I am blessed to have come from such a strong heritage that helped in the preparation for my future.

Will Holak, for your proofreading, hawk eyes, and attention to detail.

John Young, who convinced and encouraged me of the worth of this endeavor. He was a sounding board when needed during the whole process.

Foreword

I started writing this book over a decade ago but found that my story grew both in length and depth as I recorded it. I never expected it to become such a story as it has now become. At first, it was just a record of my experiences for posterity's sake. But it has become a record of God's provision and goodness—and most of all God's faithfulness.

If you had asked me thirty years ago whether I would choose the path my life has ended up taking, with youthful zeal, I probably would have said yes to some things, but with pragmatic understanding definitely no to others. That is the beauty of life when we follow and trust God. He knows best what we need and how best to glorify His name while using us. He can do this in all things that come our way, so long as we are prepared to allow Him to be who He is—God.

He does not always take us by the shortest route, however. The Israelites were only eleven days from Canaan, but because God needed them to learn certain lessons before they were ready to face the inhabitants of the land that He had promised to them, it ended up taking forty years. In the same way, it would have been easier if I did not have to go through all that I have been through, but then I would have faced many things without learning the lessons I needed to learn. So, there is no resentment toward God!

Some experiences that I have recounted in these pages were difficult—a lot of which I contributed to. When I finished high school, if a house represented my life, it was like a white-ant-ridden beach shack, pretty on the exterior but hollow and flimsy on the inside, not to mention a mess with all the sand that had been dragged in. But then God stepped in on my invitation. In the years that followed that prayer for a cleanup, my life was characterized by turmoil and a downward spiral, but two things remained constant—God's faithfulness and His love. He healed and restored broken relationships, and He rebuilt and rehabilitated a broken life while strengthening an immature faith by forcing me out of my belief system and refocusing me on Him.

As part of the rebuild, I was able to say to my family at different points that there were things I did, thought, and felt that I should not have done, thought, or felt. These were followed by the words, "I am sorry." This book is simply a testimony of God's grace and faithfulness, *not* a rehash of past events. Things could so easily have gone in a different direction. And Satan would be jumping with glee. But God did what I have learned He does best—surprise us when we least expect or deserve it. God is faithful!

Mark Elvery
May 2018

Out of the Blocks

The Race Begins

After a couple of years of abnormal feelings and unexplained behaviors from my body, I found myself sitting before a medical specialist. Between us was a large, spacious, solid-wood desk. The year was 1993. After only a few minutes of listening and jotting the occasional note, he looked up. Wearily, he shuffled the papers on which he had scrawled those rough annotations, leaned back in his antique leather office chair while resting his elbows on the armrests, and clasped his hands on an overly distinguished stomach. Then peering over the desk and without further ado, he pronounced those words that I would carry with me from that moment on: "Congratulations, you've got MS!"

We surveyed one another in silence for a moment, with neither of us prepared to open further dialogue. For me, it was a relief to hear why my body had been acting in such an erratic and unpredictable manner. And as for the doctor, I once more received his normal bedside manner, as I had first experienced years before when I had been in my final year of high school.

I simply said thank you as I rose to my feet. Without rising from the chair, he leaned forward to reach out and dismiss me from his presence with a noncommittal wave of his hand. With that, my time was up, and he half-grasped my outstretched hand with a faraway attention as he began to think about his next patient. I walked out, never to return.

When I got home, I immediately sourced another neurologist and booked an appointment. On repeating my history and the symptoms that I had observed over recent days, the diagnosis was confirmed, and the new neurologist offered some advice at no extra charge. His simple suggestion was that I should withdraw from my dental studies, as what was the point since I would inevitably never work in the dental field.

What did not add up to me was the fact that I felt God had led me into this degree in the first place—a five-year degree of which I had completed three years. Yet here I was, coming to what seemed like an abrupt dead end.

This led to the inevitable question of what I would do with this information. Jumping off a bridge was not really an option. Becoming a recluse held only marginally more appeal. One thing I did know, however—giving up was not an acceptable option for me. I reminded myself that if God had placed me in this course, He would not suddenly change His mind!

In that instant, the decision was made in my mind. *No matter how hard it gets, and whatever is needed, persevere and never give up!* An answer that had its origin long before.

* * *

These were values that I had learned during my childhood, and they came as I saw them lived out growing up in a Christian home: to work hard, keep your head down, persevere, apply yourself, and leave the rest up to God.

I do not remember the exact age (probably about six) when I chose to follow Jesus, but I remember it clearly. One evening during family devotions, it really sank in that there would be a day of reckoning for everyone when we would have to stand before God and face up to what we had done with Jesus's sacrifice, the free gift of God. There would be no hiding, and the truth of what we had or had not done would be uncovered.

It was in that moment, with childlike comprehension, that I decided that I wanted Jesus to be my best friend. I remember kneeling with my mother in front of the couch and asking Jesus to come into my heart. This gave me a warm, contented feeling, but looking back, there was not much more in that act. It was like when you pick people from a lineup to be on your team. You pick those who can best advance your objectives. My objective was to tick all the boxes in an attempt to pass any possible "entrance exam" to heaven. Nothing more. There was still something wrong in my life, but I could not put my finger on it.

In reality, I was still living for myself. My goal in life was to get away with anything and everything I could when it suited me, and to make life as easy, comfortable, and pleasurable as possible with as little guilt as possible. While I had responded to many appeals during my younger years and had received salvation, I was still immature in my faith, and my life was no better than anyone else's. And as a result, I would repeatedly let the Lord down and backslide. I really had no testimony or proof in my life that I had something different from the rest of the world. And as a result (I must admit), I was a little terror at times, trying to circumvent and take as much as I could along the way. I was in the habit of taking, not giving.

One example of this, I recall, was when my father helped to add a dining hall onto the Asia Pacific Christian Mission (APCM) campsite at the Tambourine Mountain Keswick Convention. To me, it was a giant piece of playground equipment. A giant obstacle course where I could jump over piles of floorboards, scramble under floor joists, and crawl commando style around in the red dirt. I certainly did succeed in providing a good washing challenge for my mother when we got home. Basically, I got in the way more than I should have. Rather than assisting, I played while my father worked; I had fun while he served. Essentially, at these times, I was of little help. But this also meant that from a very early age, the principle of hard work was demonstrated in practical and real ways.

It was not uncommon to spend Saturdays up at the convention site at working bees, where my father would help the caretaker with numerous maintenance and construction projects—projects such as lifting, stumping, and closing in under the caretaker's residence, starting brickwork for the machinery shed, installing guttering over the bookstall doorway, and mowing around the auditorium in preparation for biannual conventions. As kids, we would entertain ourselves on the large, sprawling grounds after only cursory contributions. He would work hard, and we would play after only working for a short period before losing focus. But these were projects that, without knowing it, instilled in me the principle of working hard and applying and offering practical help where you could.

These times also trained me in the use of my hands, something that in years to come (along with the artistic creativity involved) would be one appeal of dentistry. I must admit, it was not until later years that I was of more help at these working bees (and it would be even later before I appreciated them).

Although valuable lessons were imparted, I also used these activities to build up my sense of self-worth and self-esteem. By doing something that I felt was useful, I gained a sense of approval and appreciation. The harder I worked, the better I felt. But if I did not receive the adulation and appreciation that I thought I had earned and deserved, I was crushed.

For example, one evening I was packing up after my sister's twenty-first birthday party. We had used our local church hall to host the event. And at the conclusion, we had to remove a trailer full of tropical plants, palms, and multitudes of other equipment. By the end of the evening, I was beginning to feel somewhat nauseous. But it was a night for her, so I dug deep and carried load after load out into the inky black night. Dew was beginning to form on the tips of grass stems as my eyes became misty with emotion. Each time I turned back to any area that had good lighting, I would compose myself, wipe my eyes, and steal myself for a rapid excursion to pick up the next load before quickly departing once more into the relative seclusion of the shadows. I felt that my contribution was going unnoticed; I felt that undue sense of self-importance, despite everyone working hard, like I was making the largest sacrifice. I expected that adulation, but in fact it was time to all buckle in and just get the job done. And so we all simply worked hard until the job *was* done. Another demonstration of simply working hard.

This showed my underlying attitude. If I had to describe my early years, I would say they were volatile both emotionally and spiritually. At times, I was content and happy. At others, the best way to describe me was unsettled. I constantly responded to appeals in sermons and from itinerant preachers who came to our church, saying to God, "Hey, God, remember me? I *would* like to be your friend—honest!" My connection with God was tenuous at best—and certainly manipulative as far as I was concerned. Although I had surrendered my life to God, it was a once-only event. It had not been translated into a daily relationship. This led to recommitment after recommitment, because while I had received redemption, I felt that I had not received forgiveness so would think that I needed to go back and ask for it again and again.

If my Christian walk was a measure of my faith, it would not have been unreasonable to question the substance of that commitment that I purported to have. I would read biographies and see movies of famous Christian identities, such as Dr. Paul Brand, Dr. Paul White, and Corrie ten Boom, and dream of having an impact and testimony like these people— having a faith as solid as them and simply walking into heaven after earning that elusive pass. Such was my faulty comprehension and understanding of salvation.

It did not stop me, however, from dreaming of being a missionary doctor, working in the depths of Africa, and making huge leaps forward for the gospel. I would marry a fellow missionary nurse, and then we would have three or four children of our own before adopting several native children. These were the things that I would do.

But those years at primary school and my first years of high school were like a roller-coaster ride as my dreams would come into sharp focus before I would swerve to the left or right as I was distracted by life around me, or have the floor drop out from under me without warning when life seemed to get out of control. I would start off trying really hard to be a good Christian, which would make me feel better for a while, until I got distracted by life around me, and before I knew it, I would be back to living for myself. Along with all that came with it, including guilt, feelings of unfulfilled appreciation and worthlessness. It did not look like I would be achieving my dream anytime soon, if at all.

Then, walking home from school one day in seventh grade, my friend and I were enjoying a bright afternoon. We would jump from the footpath over the gutter onto the roadside and back again. Kicking rocks as far as we could along the gutters, it was a game to see who could get the greatest distance. Meanwhile, we kept watch for anything unusual or out of the ordinary to occupy us on the short trip home. When we came across a roadside drain, we inspected it and could see in the bottom what looked like something colorful.

We stopped, and on lifting the grill, we found four or five pages torn from a hard-core pornographic magazine. On retrieving them, we hid them in his bag, and my friend took them home with him. At first out of interest and curiosity, we would meet in secret and pull them out and look through this material repeatedly. But before I knew it, repeatedly became again and again and again. Intermittent curiosity became an all-consuming hunger. It was the only thing I thought about day and night. I could not wait to get home from school to pour over more of the same type of material. Eventually, I wanted more and more, so I went looking for it. I would do anything to get more, even if it meant shoplifting material to feed my hunger. I was becoming addicted.

To the outsider, there was nothing wrong. On the surface, I was a nice, Christian young man. But under the surface ran a strong current—a double life. I tried not to think about it because when I did, I would sink into deep remorse, guilt, and eventually depression. I would try to change things, but it never lasted long before I was sucked back in. A journey that mirrored my Christian walk. It was not a daily walk.

With this growing habit of deception and hiding my true self, one thing that I found easier as I grew up was to suppress feelings of anger or dissent, especially when there was conflict and disagreement with my parents and family. I knew that my place was to honor my parents, which I thought meant that I should never allow myself to show elevated levels of emotion. At times, this resolution failed, just like my resolutions to straighten my life out.

Other Christians had no idea of the disparity between what I said and what I did. There was little to no spiritual depth in my Christian faith, and so the emotional pressure cooker continued to develop. The only thing that kept my tenuous link with Christian things was the fun and enjoyment of social events (including youth camps) that was more appealing to me than studying the Word and allowing it to transform my life until I was confronted with reality.

In eighth grade, my childhood came to an end when my grandmother died. I distinctly remember the day of her funeral. I still went to school in the morning but then was picked up a few blocks from the school partway through the day. I had to walk to a bus shelter and wait there for my ride. As I sat there in the warm midday sun, watching the occasional car drive past on that normally bustling street that had fallen eerily quiet, I felt the butterflies in my stomach begin to rise. It was not so much the gravity of the day as it was the uncertainty of where I stood spiritually.

It proved to be with good reason. It was the first funeral I had ever attended, and I was both nervous and restless. What got me most was not the service (although hearing the hymn "Great Is Thy Faithfulness" is still emotionally significant for me to this day); it was at the graveside looking down into that deep hole and seeing a casket at the bottom and realizing that there was no way for it to come back up. It was final!

My grief was overwhelming. I knew something was not right in my life, but I did not know what I needed to do to make it right. I also was not confident in where my eternal future lay on that day when I would stand before God. I felt no security. Deep down, I knew that I had been using Him for my own benefit. I was not in any kind of real relationship with Him. I did not know what to do or how to express it, even if I had been asked. I knew that there was no way to change things once you were in that deep hole and casket. They were things that needed to be changed in the here and now, but all I did was keep on keeping on because as I saw it, that is what you did when you were part of my family. My life continued to be eaten away below the surface just like white ants eat a house. But God was about to break through in my life.

2

Rushing Wind

Be careful what you ask for.
God may just say, "Yes."

Throughout my high school years, I went to a high school camp run by Worldwide Evangelisation for Christ (WEC) where I made good friendships with other young Christian people. Without realizing it, while we were having bundles of fun, I received solid biblical teaching. Then when I was in tenth grade, God started to do something in my life. I went to yet another camp, as I had done every year throughout my high school years. But this particular year, I heard God knock on my heart's door.

The speaker that year was a man by the name of Frank McInnis, who had ironically been the speaker at a Daily Vacation Bible School (DVBS) at my childhood church where I made one of my many recommitments. What he said at this camp really got through to me. If I were to assess my life by just half of the Ten Commandments, I would fall far short of a pass mark.

- Deuteronomy 5:7 tells us that we should have no other god apart from the one true God. But I had made myself number one! - *Guilty!*
- Deuteronomy 5:16 tells us clearly to "Honor your father and your mother," but I had failed to fulfil this one totally. - *Guilty!*
- Deuteronomy 5:17 prohibits murder, yet in Matthew 5:22a, Jesus develops this further by saying, "Anyone who is angry with a brother or sister will be subject to the judgment *of murder*" [Italics added]. - *Guilty!*
- Deuteronomy 5:18 tells us not to commit adultery, yet in Matthew 5:28, Jesus again takes it deeper by saying, "Anyone who looks at

a woman lustfully has already committed adultery with her in his heart." - *Guilty!*

- Deuteronomy 5:19 tells us, "Do not steal," yet there had been many times when my light hands had pocketed small objects from school—for example, all sorts of stationery—and this extended to instances of shoplifting to get my hands on pornographic material. - *Guilty!*

So, by my own admission, I was a dishonorable, murdering, adulterous thief who lived only for himself. The only pass mark acceptable to God was perfection, and like everyone, I fell far short of this, just as it says in Romans 3:23 that "all have sinned and fallen short." And if I had broken one commandment, then I was guilty of having broken them all (Jam 2:10). God did not grade on the curve. He graded on the cross. On perfection. And I was far from perfect.

I came to realize that while you may live anonymously as just another face in the crowd, when you meet God, you face eternity alone. And that eternity would be spent in only one of two places for countless ages. In reality, I understood that my eternity would be a lost one, not an eternity in paradise. But this was where an amazing gift was on offer—the offer that Jesus would take that guilt, take my place, and take the punishment that I deserved (death, according to Romans 6:23). He had not only taken care of the punishment as an independent bystander, He had actually taken that punishment on Himself when it was taken from me and placed on Him. All for me. Before this time, I had been living for myself. Now I knew I owed my all to the God who had delivered me.

After all of my arguments, I accepted that I was part of that "all," and I could not do anything to make myself acceptable to God. Working hard could do nothing, deciding to try really, really hard in my own strength would never get me over that line, and going forward for recommitments again and again was worthless. We were told how the standard to enter God's perfect heaven is perfection, which is what keeps it perfect. And if imperfection was acceptable, then it could not be perfect by definition. I had transgressed God's laws and missed the mark, just like everyone else. And there was nothing any of us could do in response. He did it all! It is all Him. He paid the price for our downfall with His own blood. To avoid that eternity, I only needed to accept a free gift.

Jesus had not just died for the whole world, He had died for *me*. And that was the free gift. His offer was not just to me but to us all. But then it was up to me personally whether I accepted it or not. I had heard the message of the gospel many times before, but it was like I had never heard it before. It was at this point that I needed to fall at Jesus's feet to receive forgiveness. God's expectation is that I am perfect, but his other expectation is that I know Jesus. My best would never be good enough. I needed a righteousness not of my own. Jesus is perfect so that I don't have to be perfect and this is why I am acceptable.

I believed it and had responded time and time again. But I had never actually heard it in such a way as I did at that camp. It was made very clear to me, and that's when I decided to hand my life fully over to trust Jesus. I made another commitment, but this time I surrendered all, as imperfect and hamstrung as I was. I still had a lot to learn about daily submission before you could say that I gave Him everything!

It was at that camp that I embraced fully the gift of eternal life from my Savior, and I began that journey of "long obedience." Before this, I would make a decision at a children's program and think, *Now I have made it!* I accepted the gift of salvation, but I did not make it a daily walk. I thought the rest would follow, but I missed the point that spiritual life was a daily walk—a marathon.

This was a pivotal moment in my life. I felt my eternal future and destination were assured, and I stepped into the race. It was the spark that would grow into a fire. It began a strategic year in my life that was full of youthful enthusiasm and commitment. A desire grew in me to take the next step in my spiritual walk and be baptized. I felt like my life journey was on power drive. I grew closer to God and felt close to Him as well. I was serving God in every way that I could. It was the kind of year that I look back on and refer to as one of those 'best years'.

I remember, lying on my bed one afternoon six months later, listening to the Keith Green song "Rushing Wind"[1] (see appendix 1) as I read his biography, *No Compromise,*[2] about his passion to never compromise his Christian walk. I put the book aside and let the words of that song, "Rushing wind blow through this temple, Blowing out the dust within,"[3] wash over me. I thought about how I had dug myself so deep into my hypocrisy that it seemed like it was almost impossible to break free, and I found myself crying out just as Joni Eareckson Tada had done in her youth, "I'm such a hypocrite, but I don't want to be. Please, Jesus, do something in my life to turn it around."[4] I, too, from that moment desired to place my life fully into God's hands. I fell facedown on the floor in tears as my heart cried out to God to make me holy. My life was His temple, and for Him I wanted it cleaned up and cleaned out. If there was anything in my life that did not bring Him honor, I gave Him permission to do whatever He needed. Whatever it took! Never imagining what was to come.

In June 1990, eighteen months later, I arrived home after soccer training late one Friday afternoon. It had been a wet day, and I had enjoyed being able to push myself that bit harder due to the cool winter weather and play with a bit more enthusiasm, going for a few more sliding tackles than normal due to the water-logged conditions. I got home covered in mud and headed straight for the shower. As I sat on the edge of my bed pulling off my footwear, my feet were prunes—wrinkled and numb from those cold, soggy socks and poor circulation. I thought, *Yes! It was definitely cold and wet! A hot shower will certainly be nice.*

After soaking under a hot shower, I climbed out, dried myself off, and put on a warm tracksuit. I was going to add to the warmth with a pair of fleecy lined boots when I noticed that my feet were still cold and numb. *Probably due to the extreme and extended cold and wet conditions,* I thought.

But over the next two days, that numbness spread from my feet up my legs to just below my knees. On Sunday afternoon, I shared this with my parents. On doing so, they immediately sat me down on the end of their bed with my mother on one side and my father on the other. They held me and prayed over me (this was always the first port of call). After prayer, they decided to take me to our local GP the next evening (Monday). On listening to the symptoms and history, he referred me to a specialist, a neurologist in town. The first available appointment was that Friday at 11 a.m.

I continued to attend school until that appointment in preparation for my midyear exams the following week. By now, I was in my senior year of high school, endeavoring for the best possible results I could achieve, as I was hoping for a tertiary entrance (TE) score of 990 (required to do medicine— the first step in achieving my dream). So, a lot was riding on the results of those exams.

On the day of the appointment, I left school during the morning break, expecting to be back in time for lunch. On being ushered into the doctor's inner sanctum, I described the symptoms and events of the previous Friday, after which the doctor announced, "I want you in the hospital within the hour, because there could be three things causing this numbness: a brain tumor, a piece of bone that has chipped off a vertebra to be lodged in your spinal cord, or a virus of some kind. There is a 70 percent chance that it is one of the first two, so you need to get to the hospital straight away!"

This was my first exposure to his bedside manner. Do not candy coat *any* details and always say it straight, which meant that no empathy or compassion seemed evident. My stomach felt like it was in my throat and around my ankles at the same time. What was the numbness due to? Would I be okay? Did within the hour mean immediately? But more importantly, what did it all mean for my exams? It did not seem like I could put it off until after my upcoming assessments (although the thought did cross my mind). They were my whole focus (not health)!

The most amazing thing happened though. Before we walked out of his office into the reception area, I felt the peace of God wash over and through me. My mother had accompanied me to the appointment, and as we rode the elevator down to the ground floor, I found myself reassuring my now frantic mother that everything would be all right. She ran through a list of all that we would have to do, while I tried to calm the situation. ("All things work together for good," as Romans 8:28 NRSV tells us). I did not know how exactly, but I knew they would! We did not need to worry; God was not surprised, and He had it all under His control.

I asked that we call in to my school just down the road so that I could let my friends in the Interschool Christian Fellowship (ISCF) group that I attended know so that they could hold me in their prayers. I knew where my ultimate strength came from. Then we went home to throw a few things into a bag before heading back to the hospital to complete all of the admittance paperwork. After being admitted, I was subjected to over 120 x-rays, after which I was sure I was glowing! I found that this was only the beginning, as over the next week, I underwent many additional tests, including blood tests, further x-rays, CT and MRI scans, as well as a lumbar puncture.

At the close of the week, the specialist announced that he had no idea as to the cause and could only give a symptomatic diagnosis of *transverse myelitis* (swelling across the spinal cord). There was no tumor and no broken vertebrae. So, these were off the table. He had noticed a single small white dot on one MRI film but could not identify it. The best he could say was that it could be something like multiple sclerosis, but this was highly unlikely because I was "awfully young for that." He put me on a course of oral Prednisolone (a corticosteroid) to help reduce any inflammation and ordered rest.

By the time I returned to school that next week, the midyear exams were over. I had made it back just in time for the relaxing final week when we would watch movies and play games! What a major disappointment it was, as there was so much riding on all forms of assessment in that final year of school. Rather than assessment, all I got was more relaxation, which after a week in bed was definitely not needed. It also left me with the problem of gaining sufficient assessment in my senior year. I was able to sit for some makeup exams, which provided some token results. This was better than nothing, but it would be nowhere near enough. Instead, what I needed was something to take my mind off the problem of gaining sufficient assessment (games and movies were not going to do the job).

Now, during that final year of high school, I had been leading the ISCF group at my school. It can be quite isolating when other Christians at your school come from all over the city, so I thought it would be good to develop relationships between Christian students in the inner-city school zone. In that way, you may find other Christian students in your local area just attending a different school. So, I contacted different school ISCF leaders to invite them to a games afternoon in the Brisbane City Botanic Gardens. As a group, we seemed to hit it off, so much so that the year twelves decided to go together to a camp in the midyear holidays run by Scripture Union (SU) Queensland, called Discipleship Camp.

Here was that 'something' I needed to take my mind off my predicament. I decided to still go to that camp since it had been booked before that mysterious health issue and there being nothing more I could do. It took some fast talking, negotiating, and a promise to not get involved in any overly strenuous physical activities before I was able to convince my parents to allow me to attend. Together with that group of fellow year twelves, we took part in discipleship, as the camp name suggested, to grow deeper in our Christian walk while learning how to better study the Bible and even how to present short studies and sermonettes.

This was another pivotal moment in my Christian walk. I developed ongoing deep friendships with other committed young Christian people. My heart's desire to mature in the Christian faith was nurtured, and most of all, I also met my future wife there.

Little did I realize God sometimes takes us up on our sincere prayers! My prayer for a rushing wind had been sincere and come from the core of my being. He took my prayer seriously, and eighteen months later, this incident with numb feet followed by a week in the hospital had seen the onset of my multiple sclerosis (MS). Now, I am not saying that God gave me MS, but He *is* sovereign, and whatever we face in life must first be vetted, allowed, and approved by God Himself. In a way, I feel a real affinity with Job, as I picture Satan saying to God, "Let's just see what 'whatever it takes' really means!" And God saying, "All right." In this way, He answered my prayer at the same time in a way that I never anticipated, by saying, "All right."

Now, whether you want to say, the MS was sent by God, allowed by God or simply that it was the result of a broken world, I know that God used it to pull my life apart so that He could rebuild it. He maybe allowed Satan to wreak havoc, or I may have been partly responsible for what happened. I do believe it was a mixture of all of these that led to my MS and the path that my life took over the following years (the onset was just the start).

As Joni Eareckson states, "From God's perspective I believe it was an example of Hebrews 12 where a loving father will reproof and correct a wayward, unruly, and disobedient child; and bring about discipline. In the sense of discipline and restoration. Not retribution, but restoration."[5] God is in the business of restoration, not retribution. Furthermore, Satan, who is a destroyer, loves nothing more than creating chaos, disruption, and destruction in the lives of God's people. And unfortunately, in part (large or small), I was also responsible for the eventual eruption and damage to family relationships that would take place in the years to come.

But all of that does not really matter to me, as we are told in Romans 8:28 that He is able to use all circumstances for His ultimate purpose, and He can use "all things to work together for good" (Rom 8:28 NRSV). But that only means something if God is in fact good Himself. And I know that He is more than just good. So even if He allowed this, and I do believe He used it to reroute my life, I will still say, "That is okay. I will still praise Him for it." He was faithful. And He was faithful in His goodness! I can now say with Job, "Shall we accept good from God, and not trouble?" (Job 2:10), so, I jokingly say, 'Be careful what you ask God for. He may just say "Yes!"'

Another way of looking at it is that He gave me a vote of confidence by allowing the MS. He thought I was able to cope with it. Even in those early years of the disease, I could see, and today I can see even more clearly, His hand at work in the midst of a tumultuous life. And as a result, I can say that *all* things (even those things that were not good in themselves) worked for good.

3

University Life

Is the axle still at the center
of the wheel?

As far as school assessment in that final year went, I was able to apply for special consideration from the Board of Secondary School Studies due to the health problems I had encountered in my senior year. This was supposed to take care of the fact that I had missed those exams and compensate for my lack of results. Even so, my mind was not fully put to rest. I still did not know whether this would disadvantage me in attaining my desired TE score or not. I simply had to leave it in the hands of a sovereign God.

Ever since I was young, I had dreamt of being a missionary doctor. But as year eleven drew to a close, I was told in no uncertain terms by an English teacher that I would never gain a 990 TE score (the required entry score for medicine) and she had asked, "What's the point of making an effort?"

My sister had been the dux of her high school and received a 990 TE score. My brother had received a 990 TE score and was en route to receiving a university medal (awarded to top-level university students upon graduation), so I felt that I had a lot to live up to. And I was feeling inadequate to begin with. The questions constantly in my mind were, Could I match up? Was I good enough? What if I failed? Now, the comment from that teacher was devastating. It only reinforced my feelings of inadequacy. Regardless, I kept hoping and striving to be and do my best, something I had learned from observation of my parents in those childhood years.

It just so happened that during Easter of my senior year, dentistry had been suggested to me as an alternate career path. The artistic side of the profession and the use of one's hands seemed intriguing, and I immediately considered it as something that I could see myself pursuing happily for my entire working career. It was a viable alternative. But *only* an alternative.

I had six preferences to list on my university application form, and it was recommended that every one of the available preferences be used (unless you were totally confident [arrogant] of your final result—depending on your personality). So, I followed this advice, placing dentistry as my second option (medicine remained number one). When the senior results came out, I got a TE score of 980, but the cutoff for medicine was 990. And so I had missed that cutoff, but with special consideration, I was accepted into dentistry (the cutoff that year being 985). It seemed that I had been led into dentistry when the door was closed to medicine yet another alternative door had been opened especially for me.

Then, when I began the degree, I flourished with a grade point average (GPA) of 7.8 out of a possible 8 in my first year. In several subjects, I ended up in the top few places. (I was even offered a place in the English Department to complete a concurrent arts degree).

And while I thrived in my academic life, my spiritual health also flourished. I joined a Christian group called Evangelical Students (ES) where a number of friends from grade twelve who had attended those significant high school SU camps (Discipleship and Schoolies Week Camps) were also involved. We constantly encouraged and spurred each other on while regularly reminiscing about Discipleship Camp.

Once more, everything was on power drive in my life. Things had gone well in my academic life. Things were going well in my spiritual/social life. My involvement with church ministries continued in arenas such as Sunday School and the support band at my church. I also got involved with the SU beach mission at Kingscliff in northern New South Wales, where a number of my university friends also went. I found it greatly developed my skills in children's ministry while enabling me to exercise my musical skills on guitar. Quite rapidly, they recognized my gifting and eagerness to serve, and I stepped up from being a team member to a team leader, then to 2IC (second in charge) of the mission as a whole.

This was how I would spend my summer holidays. All other holidays throughout the rest of the year never seemed to coincide with school holidays; otherwise, I would have filled every moment possible with children's work. I loved the opportunity of telling children who God was and what He had done for them. It was almost as if I was trying to repeat the same things as those 'best years' in my years of high school, in the hope that it would become real and central to me once more. I had learned in those years that so long as I kept myself busy (my mind as well), then Satan would not have the opportunity presented to him to tempt or misdirect me. But now that daily walk had dropped off once again.

It was not until one such beach mission where I saw just how God can work. It took the theoretical into the practical! We had heard on the radio that a violent storm was coming in from the open sea. Our entire setup was made up of forty-year-old tents. We knew that a violent storm would decimate our campsite. With all of our equipment and personal luggage, this would be a devastating blow.

We battened down the hatches as much as we could. We had access to a church hall over the road, but there was a limit to how much we could move in time. When we had done as much as we could, all we could do was call on God for divine intervention.

I went down onto the beach with a few teammates. We stood facing the tumultuous ocean with the menacing black storm clouds before us. We could hear the wind howling over the sound of the crashing waves, but we stood our ground and called on God for help. What happened next amazed us.

The storm seemed to split in half, one half going north and the other going south. What remained above was clear sky. We were exhilarated and felt almost indestructible, although we knew that we had no part in what we had seen. We later heard that the storm cells had certainly been devastating and caused significant damage, as earlier warnings had predicted. It boggles the mind to think what damage would have been done if we had been hit. In this, what I saw was not a theoretical power of God as our prayers were answered. I saw a very real, solid example of God at work in the physical world. You would think I would be in awe of a God who could do this.

At times like this, I was full of energy, enjoying a vibrant and busy life where I rarely stopped. But it would not last. I was still living for myself, taking where I could, not walking with God daily or receiving my strength from Him. I really only had a historical Christ, not a personal savior, and so a new life was not pushing out the old. He was not the center of my life. And once more, I gained my sense of identity from doing things.

This exemplified what Isaac Watts once said, that "Satan always finds some mischief for idle hands to do."[6] And likewise, I kept myself occupied so that my mind was kept busy, so I would not find time to be distracted by other more destructive things. But this busyness ended up being misplaced. More than keeping myself occupied and succeeding in preventing idle hands, it became something that provided my self-identity. There were murky waters below the surface in my home life. And before too long, these would become obvious.

I eventually reached university, where I wanted to be treated as the adult that I felt I was. With the added freedom that comes with university life, I was feeling more and more stifled at home. I felt off balance. I was nineteen years old, yet I felt I was not trusted (which I will admit may have resulted from different deceptions being discovered in the past).

My parents had come from a strong Methodist background (of justification through faith), and as such, I was brought up with firm boundaries and rules. (Sometimes I bucked at the bit and felt the word *strict* was more in order, but now I recognize and am thankful for that firm biblical grounding that I received to make me who I am today.) As I grew older, along with my growing sense of independence, I felt that there was little relaxation of this firmness.

For so long, I had been suppressing how I felt, and eventually, it became natural for me to not only suppress but to put on a mask to keep things calm at home. As time went by, this became more and more common, and I did not know how to stop this trend and reverse it. So, it continued to develop until I simply came to accept that I acted one way at home and another way outside.

Some would say that you are who you are when you are at home. But for me, I was truly myself when I was *not* at home. I felt relaxed and able to be natural, so much so that I wore a mask when I was at home. And by this stage, this was me. It began to torment me more and more since I knew that I was compromising and being hypocritical.

That biography of Keith Green called *No Compromise* had had such an impact on me in grade ten, yet here I was compromising myself and who I claimed to be. Things were not right. The only thing was that I did not know how to rectify the issue, so I just kept ignoring it as best I could. Once more, as in years past, no one knew how much I was being torn apart inside. One thing was certain: a storm was brewing. And the intensity grew stronger until things finally erupted in a way that I would not be able to control.

4

The Storm

God is good all the time,
and all the time, God is good
—Even when it does not feel like it.

After beginning to view pornography in grade seven, my conscience slowly started to become tangled. The water became murkier and murkier. And as a result, I was haunted by it for years to come, until I came to fully recognize how much it disrespected the women involved, myself, my future wife, and God. Eventually, I came to understand how in later life this could and would affect marriage relationships and how the images involved were far from realistic with all the airbrushing and unrealistic body forms. But when I was younger, I did not recognize this, so these issues did not even cross my thought processes.

There would be times when I would try to overcome these temptations by means of my own willpower, but I had been hooked well and truly. So, when some magazines were found in my room years later, it simply showed that I had not been able to conquer this temptation as I had professed. After this, I felt I was never able to regain the trust of my parents. I was torn up within myself. All I felt was shame, scorn for myself, and disappointment that I had let both them and the family name down. Notwithstanding how I had let both myself and God down as well. So much for no compromise!

I felt at the time that the support and encouragement that I needed to help me beat this temptation was not there. In fact, I did not know what I needed; my life was in such turmoil. To be fair to them, they did the best they could; if I did not know what was needed, how could they? Looking back on things, what I needed was to get my life right with God first, and then second, hand it all over to Him. And they could not have helped me in this respect. I and only I was able to take those steps that would allow Him to take over and help me beat this temptation.

At the same time, over the years, I found it easier to make sure I did not initiate any emotional scenes because I would be unable to express well in spoken words what I was feeling if a scene were to ever arise. My mind was much clearer when I could take my time and select my words while writing rather than talking. So, I would resort to suppressing my feelings instead and staying silent. I have heard it described as 'learning the language of silence'. Rather than talking things out, I would internalize, and as a result, this suppressed pressure began to build and continued to do so, preparing the way for an uncontrolled release. It was not a matter of if but when.

This only became more accentuated once I started university. In my first year, I broke up with my high school girlfriend and the following year began dating a girl a year below me at the same university. Deep down, I was looking for a sense of self-worth and approval with someone to look up to and admire me. I was looking to solve that issue of low self-confidence and self-esteem.

I found that this girl's parents treated me like the adult that I felt I was. It was partly the warm glow of love as well as the fact that I had become more relaxed when not at home, but I always enjoyed spending time over at her house, while my own home life was deteriorating rapidly.

At the end of my second year of university, my parents sat me down to reprimand me for not focusing on my studies despite me maintaining my grades at a relatively high level. My mother did a lot of the talking on this particular night. My father normally was quite reserved, and this occasion was no different. I would describe him as having a quiet strength, where he chose his words carefully, and when he did speak in times like this, you knew that he held strong feelings. So when he spoke, I knew to listen even if I did not follow his advice.

After all was said and done, I was shaken. I did not know what I could do to satisfy them short of ending the relationship, which I was definitely unwilling to do. After all, I was in love. I felt inadequate, and I felt myself beginning to shut down emotionally. I went and lay on my bed until I heard the rest of the house grow quiet after everyone went to bed. I snuck out and headed down to a phone box one street over behind the house to ring my then girlfriend.

I ended up having a long conversation with her mother since she had also retired. I was encouraged to take a deep breath, calm down, and at least accept this situation until I turned twenty-one years of age (just over a year away). Then, if I still wished to leave home, I could do so as an adult. That settled me down and gave me a renewed sense of patience. As I snuck back in, I was careful not to make any sound as I climbed the stairs. I went to bed expecting that dawn would bring some improvement. Remember—dawn always brings a new day and a new beginning. But a storm was on its way and would arrive sooner than I expected.

My twentieth birthday began like any other Saturday, except I had to work at the part-time job I had secured the year before. After coming home, I quickly mowed our next-door neighbor's yard, an old spinster who had paid me to mow her lawn for years.

Afterward, I showered to cool down and clean up before changing into some comfortable clothes and going downstairs. With the heat, I had chosen a T-shirt that had seen better days but was a cool and comfortable old favorite from an ISCF camp in grade eight. Simply by wearing it, I was reminded of happier, more carefree days. It was one of those cozy yet comfortable threadbare clothes that you find hard to toss out.

When my mother saw it, she ordered me to "march right back upstairs", take it off, put on something else, and put "that old rag" in the bin. I began to protest that it was my favorite shirt and that I just wanted to relax a bit before dinner. But before I could say anything more in its defense, she grabbed the shirt to stop me as I began to walk off. It was so threadbare that it began to tear. I naturally twisted away in a futile attempt to save it, which only succeeded in tearing it further.

One thing led to another, things escalated, and my father was called in. Before I knew it, something snapped within me. I was shocked at the emotions surfacing. At the same time, I was both upset and furious. All of that suppressed frustration and anger erupted. The *if* became real, and the *when* became now. The pressure was released, and in that instant I knew I had to get out of there before I did (or said) something I would never be able to take back.

Turning, I found myself screaming, "That's it!" as I ran for my room. I knew exactly what I was going to do the instant my foot hit that first step that led up the flight of stairs I had snuck up so quietly just weeks before. There was no concern about being silent now. I had to go anywhere other than there to deal with everything that was going on in my life. Once I locked the door, I pulled out some bags and began to throw some bare essentials in them. All the while, my parents stood at my locked door yelling, pleading, screaming, demanding, even threatening that I open it and talk. But I was too far gone.

I stuffed the bare essentials into those bags—one with good clothes for university and church, a sports bag with my university textbooks and notes, a knapsack with some casual clothes, my briefcase with my Sunday School material (I was teaching a grade-five Sunday School class at the time), and a roll of song sheets. Once finished, I pulled the fly screen off the second-floor patio outside my room before throwing my packed bags down to the back lawn one at a time. When all of these were waiting for me on the back lawn, I unlocked my door and used my guitar case as a battering ram to push past my parents down the stairs.

When they saw that I was serious, their cries turned into hysterical pleading and begging. On reaching the kitchen, my mother appealed, trying to dissuade me by saying, "But I've made a special birthday dinner for you. At least sit down and eat so we can talk." The damage had been done though, and there was no going back. I simply had to get out of there. I exited through the back door and proceeded out on to the back lawn where I gathered up the bags. When I had retrieved everything, I set off, stumbling down to the back fence under the weight of this pile of luggage before I awkwardly half-climbed, half-fell over that last obstacle. But once this barrier was behind me, I made my way down to the street where I had made that secret phone call a few weeks previously.

Despite being in a state of distress, I was still able to think and plan ahead. I knew that my first step would be to call my girlfriend, but I realized she would unlikely be able to drop everything and be there instantly even if she happened to be available. There would still be a wait, and I did not want to sit there indefinitely, so I proceeded to walk on to the next telephone booth.

This meant I had to climb a long hill with the sports bag on my chest, my knapsack on my back, a larger bag in my left hand (the song roll between the handles), and my guitar and briefcase in my right hand. I must have looked a sight—essentially a two-legged pile of luggage slowly waddling up the hill. My entire earthly possessions held awkwardly in a ball, with me at its core.

And so I ran. And I would continue to run for the next five years. It became my default reaction whenever things became too much for me to handle emotionally. It was easier to run than to sit down and deal with any issue that arose.

5

Run, Run, Run!

When you harbor bitterness,
happiness docks elsewhere.

I eventually reached that next phone booth a kilometer away where I rang my girlfriend. I asked if she would come and pick me up, and then I just sat down on the footpath and simply waited for her to come. With nowhere else for me to go, she took me to her home. I was such a wreck that when her mother gave me a hug upon walking through the door, all I could stammer in a faltering voice was, "I tried, but I just can't do it!"

I couch-surfed (as they call it) there for the next three weeks while the pastor of our church tried to mediate the situation. But whenever we all sat down in the same room, emotions were so raw it would turn into an outright verbal battle before anything could be achieved. I was a tangled ball of emotions, full of anger, jealousy, guilt, sorrow, grief, confusion, weakness, and need. Every emotion that had been suppressed was released in a tidal wave, causing collateral damage wherever and however it swept by. In addition, my belief system had been so rocked that no longer was life stable. And this included every relationship I had.

My emotions were such a mess that neither myself nor anyone else would be able to unravel them overnight. In fact, it took nearly twelve years before things were fully untangled. My faith was never lost, however, which I attribute to my upbringing and to the lessons that had been imparted to me in those early years; they helped to prepare me unawares for the future. I could only clutch onto what I knew to be true—God is still good, and I was still His. But the relationship with my family had taken a direct hit and would not be restored for years to come.

That pastor was still good to me, as he allowed me to move on and crash at his house for about two weeks, while we searched for a place for me to live. There was no way I could return home, so we had to find alternate arrangements. He recognized the broken relationship in my family and endeavored to seek reconciliation while working within the limits that were present. My parents, from that moment as I saw it, seemed to lose respect for that pastor, and it seemed he was criticized more often than not. Eventually, mediations broke down, and I was able to occupy a granny flat below a family from our church. I was able to share this with another young man from Townsville in Queensland, who came down to Brisbane for university study. I never had to deal with the rental agency, which suited me (but for the sake of clarity, I regarded them as my landlords). Then the slow process of reconciliation began. And slowly but surely, ground was regained in our relationship over the following years.

I was able to retrieve my ten-speed road bike so that I could get around. Without a car, this was my only means of transportation and so became vital. But it was starting to get cold at night, and I would have to leave my pastor's house at about 6:30 in the morning and ride over to my girlfriend's house, where I would get a lift to near the university in order to catch a bus in time for my first lecture. At that time of year, it was not uncommon to find frost on small pockets of ground. It was a suburb snuggled away in the foothills of the mountain range west of the city and was notorious for cold temperatures, meaning ice needed to be scraped off windscreens before early departures. So, on visiting a flea market, I bought a pair of secondhand lady's dress gloves. I then cut off the beads and fingertips to make a pair of fingerless riding gloves to wear (I could not afford to buy the real thing).

My bike became critical to survival, as it enabled my only source of income generation in those early days—my part-time weekend job at Woolloongabba on the other side of the city some twenty kilometers away. Every Saturday, I would leave on my bike for a 7:30 start in the morning and then ride home after the 5:00 p.m. close of business. In the winter months, I left before dawn and got home after dark, cold, tired, and hungry.

In those early days, I needed to put this effort in regardless of any discomfort, to at least earn enough to live. A little later, I received a small increase in my student support payment since I was no longer living at home. This would help a little but was still insufficient on its own, so I needed to work a part-time job in order to live—frugally, but at least I was able to pay the bills. Such was life when I was on my own. I was well aware that no longer were there the small comforts of living at home.

One example of this came six months after I left home. I got back to my granny flat one Saturday after working all day, just as the sun slipped below the distant horizon. Streetlights had come on, and cars needed their headlights. I pulled up outside the open door, glad to be back home after a long and busy day. I was tired, but my exhaustion had to be ignored as my mind turned to what nourishment I could come up with for dinner. It was not a case of dinner being laid out before you upon arriving home. My flat mate was sitting at a table eating his own dinner, with the door open.

As I pulled up, I went to lift my left foot off over the bike to dismount. But instead of gracefully dismounting, I tumbled back onto the concrete like a tree being felled. I ended up flat on my back with my arms and legs tangled in the bike. It was unclear where the bike and I started. It was a mass of arms, legs, wheels, and pedals. My flat mate ran out to help unpack the jumbled mess.

On dismantling the pile of metal and flesh, he checked that I was okay, and we had a good laugh about it. I was glad that he had been there, but I quickly shrugged it off with thoughts of, *Boy, you are so unfit! Stick at it, and a bit more riding should improve it.* I thought it was just a case of enduring the pain of being unfit until my fitness level increased and exercise (i.e. riding) became easier and more pleasurable, so I increased the bike riding as much as possible.

I had always found it comforting to come home to someone in the flat. And after a few months, I began to steady myself emotionally, but then my flat mate moved out, and when I stayed on, I found myself on my own with plenty of time to think. In those early days of living on my own, it was lonely and strange coming home to an empty room (that is all it basically was). There was no television, radio, or stereo, as I did not want to cause issues with my landlord.

I would get home late, after dark (the norm nearly every day of the week), unlock the door, walk in, put down my bags, and have a simple dinner. I ate simply to give my body sufficient nutrition, not for flavor or taste. I rarely ate for pleasure. Then I would sit quietly in a lone lounge chair (which had been supplied with the flat) journaling or reading until climbing into bed. It was a peaceful and quiet existence apart from those occasions that reminded me that I was no longer in the comfort of my childhood home.

One night, I arrived home at the end of a long day at the university to a cold, dark flat. I was tired and felt on the edge of mental, emotional, and physical collapse. I cooked another one-dish dinner in silence, sat down to eat, washed up, and then walked a short three meters to take a seat for yet another quiet and lonely evening.

I would sit cross-legged in an ugly, stiff-as-a-board, bright red vinyl lounge chair to gain some measure of comfort before I continued writing in my journal. I had started this shortly after I left home in an attempt to help get my head straight and process my thoughts. I found that, as always, my best thinking was done as I wrote it down on paper. On this particular night, I picked up my pen and journal and sat to begin writing, but nothing came.

After a few minutes of loud silence, I simply opened up and started to pray. I pleaded with God to show Himself. I had come to the end of my tether, and I knew it. After months of struggling, I had exhausted both my emotions and physical stamina. The only way forward would be with Him, but there was silence. It felt like He was either oblivious to or ignoring my prayers. No matter what I said, how I said it, or what I was going through, there was no response. So I called all the louder. And then God showed Himself to be faithful to answer my desperate prayer that night in a special way. I recorded what happened next in my journal.

September 15, 1993

Stopping and asking God—"What can You say to me to encourage me? I'm not moving until I hear you." [But] before the words were out of my mouth and I had time to focus my thoughts, three simple words formed in my mind. Then I realized the significance of those words—"*You Are Mine*"

You—One small person in the whole of the world and history.

Are—Not sometimes but constantly in the good and bad times. In the highs and lows. In the past, the present, and the future.

Mine—I'm not my own. I'm bought with the blood of the Lamb, and with that comes privileges—respect, position, love, and grace.

I was rebuking myself for letting unfocused thoughts flow through my mind before realizing that they had not been my thoughts. They were a message. Never before had I so clearly had God speak into my life, and it has been repeated only on a few occasions since. It was groundbreaking for me, as I felt the Lord embracing, reassuring, and encouraging me in a way that I could almost touch.

6

Congratulations

An opportunity to watch God
at work in and despite circumstances.

The first twelve months after leaving home were full of highs and lows.
There were times when I certainly hit the lows, but there were also moments
when I could feel God's arms around me or people who were used as His
instruments to encourage me. These would take me by surprise and pick
me right back up again. But more often than not, it was a case of the
mundane daily task of making ends meet and surviving.

One such example of encouragement occurred just before my flat mate
moved out and I was left on my own in the granny flat. One lady who had
been a teacher at my high school lived nearby. Her marriage had broken
down after the death of their infant son (an only child). She became a good
friend, so when she asked me to house-sit for her, I accepted to give my flat
mate some space to pack his things. When I arrived, I was presented with
two full boxes of crockery and kitchen utensils still in their packaging. She
told me that they were extras and that she would never use them, so they
were mine if I wanted them. I never did find out whether they truly were
surplus or whether she had gone out specifically to buy them for me. I still
wonder.

It was a crunch time, and I would find out whether I had it within me
to be independent or not. Life did go on after I was left on my own, and I
continued to push my bike riding to get my fitness levels up. Although, as
time went by, riding the bike did not seem to get any easier.

A short while later, my girlfriend and I asked to be dropped off one
morning at Toowong Shopping Centre so that we could walk to the
university at St. Lucia (about three kilometers away). One aim was to use
the walk as another way to work on improving my fitness level. There was

a bus, but I did not want to admit that I could not afford the fare. So, I thought I could achieve my aim of improving fitness while saving the cost of a bus fare. I could kill two birds with one stone.

We struck out on what was meant to be a relaxing, leisurely, one-hour walk, but as we progressed, I got weaker and weaker. My feet became heavier and heavier. They began to drag, and basically, it became a three-kilometer footslog. As I slowed down, I repeated with bravado that I had wanted to have a leisurely (a nice, *slow*) stroll, but for the last kilometer, my arm ended up over her shoulders, as she had to support my full weight. Just after we crossed onto the university grounds, I collapsed on the lawn, admitting that I needed to sit down and catch my breath.

Instead of arriving with plenty of time before my first lecture, I ended up in danger of not making it at all. There was little time to spare, but I could not go any farther. As we sat there, with me puffing, nothing was said except some excuse about being *really* unfit. Needless to say, I never attempted it again but made sure I had the money for the fare, even if I had to cut back on my groceries. Like exercise, hunger hurts at first, but once you break through the wall, it's not that bad.

As the year progressed, my fitness levels didn't seem to improve, no matter what I did. They were always lacking. My legs began to feel like jelly by the end of my ride home after work each Saturday. There was a certain hill near my flat that I would use to gauge whether my fitness levels were improving. Even when I used the hill before it to give me a long run up, during which I would reach speeds of up to 40 km/hr, I would still not have enough momentum to climb that final hill. I would invariably have to dismount and push my bike up the last few meters. At those speeds, it was a good thing that I never misjudged my line of travel to cross into a pothole or crack in the asphalt.

I became suspicious of some balance problems and occasional double vision that I had been having along with the fatigue. There was even one occasion when I was standing talking on a flat concrete path. And the next thing I knew, I was flat on my back on the grass beside the path. I made excuses about an old soccer injury that had given me a weak ankle. I made a joke about it, but I was secretly concerned. At the end of that year when there was one thing after another that had not been right, I decided that I would forfeit the money even though I needed it for food and pay the high fee to go see the neurologist who had treated me in the last year of high school to see if he could shed any light on the matter. So, as soon as my end-of-year exams were over, I made an appointment and went to see him. I described my symptoms, while he made some notes in my chart, after which in a matter-of-fact voice he announced that I had MS. His exact words: "Congratulations, you've got MS!"

I was not shocked, angry, scared, or anything else. I was just relieved to know that these symptoms were not imagined, and there was a good reason for both them and my poor fitness. It was validation for those things that I knew were not right. We shook hands, but despite saying, "Thank you!" my mind was made up to never return. Although I appreciated a definite answer, as I left to begin the long, slow trip home on public transportation, I reminisced about how his bedside manner had never struck me as being caring, compassionate, or confidence inspiring over the past years whenever I had seen him. It was almost as if he was proud that he had worked out the answer to the mystery. Do not worry about any empathy though! Rather than explain what he had found and why he had come to this conclusion, it seemed I was expected to simply accept his verdict without question. I knew that I did not need that form of support with a diagnosis like that. I would need God to be with me every step from now on.

Something that I would have trouble reconciling though was when another specialist soon afterward advised me to drop out of dentistry since, "I had no long-term future in this field"; so it was better to forget it and retrain now. I had miraculously been admitted into dentistry three years earlier, and I was over halfway through the five-year course. So, I naturally had to ask myself the question, "Why would God have put me here if He would then turn around and change His mind?"

I knew from the letter to the Hebrews that God is the same, "yesterday, today and forever" (Heb 13:8), so my answer to this question was to just trust that God is constant and sovereign. Circumstances may not make sense, but God is always stable. Even though we may never understand why God does certain things at certain times in certain ways this side of eternity, we have to simply trust that He is in control. And there are two things I know for certain: God can be relied upon to be faithful and good, *and* He is sovereign. Hence my joke when I say to people, "If you can work out why God would put me in a course to be trained in a profession that I would never work in, let me know!"

I am reminded of the words of Isaiah when he says, "For my thoughts are not your thoughts, neither are your ways my ways, declares the Lord" (Isa 55:8). Another way of putting it is that God can do whatever He wishes with whomever He chooses whenever He pleases. He is God; we are not! That is what I simply trust and believe. Sometimes people say, "I can't believe in a God who would allow X to happen!" But this is exactly the point; we *cannot* comprehend God, even if we tried. Sometimes, for a particular thing to make sense at all (and sometimes it does not), we have to believe in a God who is what we call sovereign! And some people are repulsed when they have no option but to do so.

We cannot comprehend an incomprehensible God—an all-wise, all-good, and all-powerful God. Timothy Keller illustrates this well in his book, *Walking with God Through Pain and Suffering*,[7] when he discusses Elisabeth Elliott's comments in her book about young children being expected to trust adults when they cannot possibly understand the hows or whys of certain directions they are given, and how as modern people, we can be horrified when we are asked to trust in a God who cannot be understood fully. Yet that is the God that we worship. Otherwise, He would not be worthy of that very worship. So, what else can we do when we do not understand? It has been said, "Sometimes God permits that which he hates, to accomplish that which he loves."[8] And it is at these times when we need to hold His hand and push on, which is exactly what I chose to do in my life from that moment forward.

Nowadays, I can confidently say that my original neurologist, without realizing it, summed it up perfectly when he said, "Congratulations" because I have had the opportunity to take a front-row seat to see a sovereign God at work. I must admit though that I sometimes have had trouble understanding His reasons and plans. I like order and to understand how and why A leads to B. I do not feel comfortable when A does not lead to B, or worse still if B leads to A. I just had to trust in what I knew, not in what I felt.

Despite a positive diagnosis, life went on as I kept trusting in a God who was in control. It had taken a while after leaving home, but finally, I was settling into an even rhythm in life. I even felt that I could continue indefinitely, despite this news. But life rarely stays static at the best of times.

It was a truth that I would become familiar with in the years to come, especially when it came to my MS (starting here). As soon as I got used to a certain level of disability, there would be another relapse, and the resultant change in my health would be such that my physical abilities were further reduced to a lower level, and I would have to start getting used to a whole new level of disability all over again. You never get stuck in a rut when you have MS because things are always changing!

Alzheimer's disease has been referred to as "the slow good night," and while in no way should this be downplayed, MS can be referred to as "the slow shutdown." Just as when your computer shuts down and programs close one by one, the transmission of signals along wires progressively falls silent until eventually signals cease altogether and the computer will neither listen to nor communicate with you. It becomes a giant paperweight on the corner of the table. In the same way, with MS, slowly but surely, physical capabilities blur with disability, and ultimately you are overrun by it and become a giant paperweight.

7

If it Rains, it Pours

Stop listening to yourself
and start talking!

I had and still have a real peace surrounding my diagnosis. I have seen and experienced His grace. God wants *so* much to bless us with His grace both in eternity and right now here on earth. I saw it when I finished high school. I saw it when I left home. I saw it in my studies. And now, I was to see it following my diagnosis, even when He protected my life leading up to that diagnosis.

A while after I began life on my own, I was still riding my bike as my only means of transport. One day, I was riding over to a friend's house. On the way, I cut the corner across a street at the bottom of a hill. I was traveling at about thirty kilometers per hour when a car emerged out of the side street that I was turning into. I tried to swing back into the road but only ended up colliding with his front left corner and was catapulted over the bonnet into the street on the other side of the car.

Sitting up in the middle of the street, I quickly did a self-assessment for any broken bones. Fortunately, the broken bone count was nil, but I was still a mess, and more importantly, my bike was a write off. I never knew that wheels on a bike could be bent at right angles in three different directions at the same time. Fortunately, I was still walking (just grazes, scrapes, and scratches all over my face and body). We were able to settle the matter out of court since he had only minor damage but I had lost my only means of transport. Like paper-scissors-rock, a car beats a bike every time! My bike had lost against the car, but providentially, it did not go so far as to mean that my life had been lost as well.

That put an end to my bike-riding days, which was not necessarily a bad thing, considering there was nothing I could have done to improve my fitness levels. This accident helped me realize that no matter what I did, riding the bike was not getting any easier and would not be safe in the long term. It was this accident that actually prompted the visit to the neurologist who broke the news of the MS to me.

I was able to take out a loan from my government student payment scheme to purchase an old Toyota Corolla Coupe. It was a bomb, which went through a liter of oil almost every month, but it was the best I could afford as my first car. I had upgraded from a pushbike to a road-worthy bomb. Things were on the up!

As much as my diagnosis, accident, and need to make a car purchase had not been disturbing to me, what was about to follow would make up for these. It was something that sent me into a tailspin a few months after my diagnosis.

I will never forget how one day at the end of those holidays, I was cleaning up around the flat before a new year of university study began. My then girlfriend appeared at the flat door unannounced and without delay told me that, as a couple, we were through. She could see no future for us. And just like that, I was single. Now I truly was on my own. There was no chance for any discussion or last-minute reconsideration. The decision had been made. And it was final.

I was so devastated that all I could do was do what I had learned to do as my default response, and ran. Leaving her to lock up the flat, I left, got in my new car, and drove. I did not care where. I just drove and drove. Fortunately, I had a full tank of fuel, so I would not have to walk in to pay for fuel with a tear-streaked face, adding to my humiliation.

Eventually, I settled down and returned well after dark. After laying a single rose at her door as a peace offering for the way I had walked out and anything I had ever done or not done, I returned home to a dark, empty flat and climbed into bed without dinner (I was nowhere near hungry) or changing to spend a restless night tossing and turning.

Then, a few days later, it began to rain and rain and rain. Not just light rain but a heavy, continual downpour. Not the best circumstance to occur during a bout of despondency and depression (which on its own wreaked enough havoc). Later I was to be diagnosed with mild clinical depression and began a course of medication. But for now, I felt worse and worse with every drop of water that fell from those heavy clouds. I began to dwell on all that I had lost—my family, my health, my career, and now my girlfriend.

I felt very much alone and suspecting that I had lost everything. This was possibly the lowest of the low points I would experience.

It rained for the next few days, and by the end, I was feeling a strong case of cabin fever. I felt like I just needed to get some fresh air, so I went out for a walk despite the rain. I took no umbrella. I did not care about getting wet! I just started walking and headed toward a local reserve.

As I walked, I just wanted to lie down and end it all, but I did not have the courage to end my life. I knew it was wrong for me to tell God that I thought He had made a mistake in allowing my life to end up this way, before ending it unilaterally! So, I thought to myself, *What if someone else did it for me?* I found myself stepping off the footpath into the street as I walked. I was thinking, *Visibility is low, and there are lots of blind corners. It would not take much for a car to come around a corner and, with the wet road, be unable to stop.* It was a selfish way to end it and possibly painful as well if death was not instantaneous. It was definitely an unpredictable way to end my life, but I was past caring.

It was not until a car finally came around a corner (but was able to swerve around me) while aggressively sounding their horn that I was jolted back into reality. I was being both a coward and selfish, but more than that, where was my trust in God? Did He not love me and care for me? Was He not faithful? Had He not been so again and again and again? Had I not been paying attention?

It had been so apparent in my life, yet here I was saying that I was on my own with everything lost. But, no! I was focusing solely on myself. I still had breath, I still had a God who loved me, and my God was indeed faithful. And that *was* enough. It was time to show a bit of faithfulness in return. If I could not hold on, I would let God hold onto me! It is a weird sensation when you start lecturing and berating yourself.

I stopped listening to myself and started listing that which I knew. From that moment, the rain became a refreshing shower. I stepped back onto the footpath and turned back toward the flat. As I walked through the rain, I continued to lecture myself, and this became more of a motivational speech. I reminded myself of where I stood as a child of God, what He had done for me and what He was doing for me in that very moment.

I was finally on my own, which was a bit daunting. However, I look back nowadays and realize it was needed to make me stand on my own two feet. I needed to let go and hold onto God in those days. Before then, I had been relying too heavily on other people, not on God. Now, He was able to help me stand on those feet while teaching me the lessons I needed to learn. It was like when a toddler clings to your leg to be able to stand. In those low times, God was still faithful. And He allowed me to cling to His leg.

In the days that followed, it was as if, to learn the lessons that God had for me, I needed to step out of my comfort zone across the deep chasm of failure. Continuing the baby analogy, it was sort of like when they start to walk. You can see that they can do it, but the confidence is not there yet. This was me. I just kept telling myself that I would get there if my eyes remained fixed on God. I did not need to rely on any human, as I had done so previously.

Trust in anyone other than God Himself, and this will inevitably lead to disappointment because no one can meet all of our expectations and needs. Sometimes we place more confidence in people than in God. Yet there is no comparison as far as who we can rely on. It was a lesson that I needed to learn—that sometimes we need to let go and let God!

In the coming months, slowly but surely, I began to come to terms with my single life, my MS, and the need to rely on God in all things. The next thing in order of priority that I needed to focus on was my study. I went on, and at the end of the semester, I sat my exams. I hoped confidence would come later, but for now, I just needed to pass; that would be enough. A baby takes small steps first remember. After those exams, I noted in my journal, "I've leant on others, but this time I have done it all by myself. That is not taking into account God's part in it. I just went at it, tried and trusted."

Shortly after this, I got my results, and yet again, He had not let me go. I passed! My new single life, far from being the end, continued on with me being able to maintain my grade point average (GPA), which was also a testimony to my upbringing, which had taught me to just get on, apply yourself, and do your best despite any distractions around you. I still felt off balance though, as for me to step out without any support of any kind was a big step. I was truly flying solo, or so it felt at times. But needless to say, God was with me and was faithful to help me even after I was left on my own.

So, when an opportunity arose to share with a counselor at the University Student Union as a referral from my doctor concerning my depression, I was able to tell her that my MS was only part of my story. I proceeded to relate the previous few years leading up to my diagnosis and current state of health. At the end, I was able to smile and say, "But you get that!" She was shocked that I could say that so casually after what she referred to as "an emotionally tensioned time."

I had originally gone to talk about my depression, but in the end, I was able to share with her my only hope. The Lord was the only one who brought me through, and He had always provided for me when I had need. I added that without Him, I would have caved in both emotionally and mentally. But He had been faithful.

Years later, I came across an account related by Doris van Stone in her book *Dorie: The Girl Nobody Loved*. It recounts an episode that parallels my experience of sharing with that university counsellor. She said, "A child psychologist came to me after I had shared my testimony in a meeting and said, 'Dorie, there isn't a reason in the world why you are not an emotional vegetable.' Then she paused and added, 'except for the grace of God.'"[9]

It showed me the way my story could be used by God despite the chaos in which I had found myself. There is no event in one's life that is pointless or useless when that life is handed over to God. God had been faithful in looking after me both physically and emotionally in not letting me go. I too could eventually testify to God's faithfulness before others, as I had even been able to say to the counsellor at the university, "You get that," before sharing my faith.

And it was all by the grace of God.

8

Pebbles in the Shoe

It is often the small things that irritate the most.

Despite God's faithfulness and the way He sustained me, repeatedly there were still times when those destructive impulses of the past once more shone through to haunt me. One example of this came on the first Saturday after I had purchased my new car. I parked it out on the vacant drive at my granny flat (my landlord had no car) and proceeded to clean the boot and interior. I was so proud of it. Later, I received a stern comment about getting up so early to make a racket below their window.

There seemed to be small issues that often kept niggling and popping up with my landlord. I tried to be a good tenant and tried to be friendly, but it seemed that there was continual underlying tension that neither side acknowledged or addressed. I just found it easier to slip into my old habit of suppression, despite knowing from past experience just how pressure can grow and may be released down the track.

In this new season of single life, it seemed that the lows were a bit more frequent than the highs, and I would have little notice before they came across my path. At these times, old habits that I had developed were even more prone to surface during pressure, such as one instance when I got home from work one very wet Saturday. Fortunately, I had finished early on this particular day, so there was still daylight when I drove in.

It had been raining heavily and steadily all afternoon, so as I walked around the corner of the house, I should not have been, but I was still surprised nonetheless to find water half a meter up the front door of my granny flat. The sod had recently been turned on a new housing development behind our property, and the problem was that the water was presently running down off the bare vacant lots across the backyard and into the paved entertainment area outside my flat door.

Fortunately, the week previously, I had repainted the back door and placed a false threshold under the door to close a two-centimeter gap. It had been an attempt to help seal/insulate the door before things turned cold in the coming winter once again. I do not know why the thought had occurred to me; I can only put it down to a God-thing! I had not been able to place silicon under the threshold as planned when my impromptu work had been halted since I had not sought permission from my landlord beforehand. So as a result, water was still seeping in at a significant rate, but at least it was not flowing into the flat freely, as it would otherwise have done.

I was frantic because the only furniture I had been able to afford was chipboard, and I knew that the slightest bit of moisture would destroy it. A window had been left ajar above my bed to allow fresh air in. So, to gain access without opening the door, to allow me to at least lift up some of my furniture, I began to remove a fly screen. But before I could fully remove it, my landlord walked around the corner and demanded to know what I was doing breaking in.

I explained that the window had been left ajar and that I feared for my furniture. I assured him that I knew what I was doing, and I promised to pay for any damage, but I was going in regardless. He did not approve of my plan, but true to my word, I did not wait. With that, I removed the screen and climbed in through the window before he could protest further. It was definitely not helpful for the landlord-tenant relationship. But in the end, I was able to save all of my furniture. Nothing was damaged (including the window), although the carpets did need a thorough drying out for several days as a result of water damage from water seeping under the incomplete false threshold.

I could be stubborn. If my mind was made up, I would force my will into action regardless of collateral damage. For years, I had submitted to my parents, as I was told to in scripture, but now I was able to exert my will regardless of someone saying to me that they did not want me to do something (e.g. climbing through an open window) that I felt was both necessary and beneficial. But it was the way that it was executed that was my old self surfacing again. The pebble in the shoe was needling once more. It had not been removed.

In instances like this, despite feeling like I was put off balance, the Lord never ceased to care for and cradle me. He would encourage me through books, the Word of God, people, and at one point, He Himself even reminded me of what I meant to Him (see "Run, Run, Run," chapter 5). It seemed like there would be a constant flow of issues when I would need His strength, input, and deliverance. This gave me strength when I needed it most. It would have been better to remove the pebble in the first place, but instead it would need regular relief. I was a slow learner, and this would not happen for a few more years.

Another instance of niggling occurred a few weeks later when it began to rain yet again. I had been to the doctors to get an ingrown toenail removed. The anesthetic was still acting, so when I got home, I headed out to the rear boundary line to dig a trench in the downpour to divert water before flooding once more resulted. I did not have a shovel, so I asked my landlord if I could borrow his if he had one. He just said, "What's the point?" Which just made me even more determined, since it was obvious what happened in heavy rain, and it was my furniture at risk. After he told me that one was kept out in the garden shed, I simply marched out, retrieved it, and began to dig that trench along the fence line on my own.

In an attempt to protect my foot, I tied a couple of shopping bags around the bandaged limb. By the end, the anesthetic was starting to wear off, and my foot was throbbing. I just had to push through the pain and keep digging to finish the job. In the end, water was successfully diverted. Most of all, thankfully, there was no leakage through the bags, so I avoided any infection. Once more, a small step.

A few days later, I was out assessing the trench when I saw my father arrive (most likely to see how I was doing with all the rain). I was quite emotional at the time, feeling beaten up and trodden down. It seemed that if I was to achieve anything as far as the drainage issue went, I would have to take care of it myself. I resented the fact that I had been left to sort it out alone without any tangible assistance. I felt myself slipping back into a depressive feeling of isolation. I felt like I was on my own in life and study, and at the same time, I felt somewhat separated from my family. Out of resentment, I thought that I would show them and do it myself! With a sore foot to boot (excuse the pun!), I was definitely feeling sorry for myself, and I just was not up to talking. So, despite the flat being open, I found it easier to once more slip into previous behavior, let the pebble niggle, and run (or in this case hide). I am ashamed to admit that I immediately hit the ground and took cover in a grove of trees about five meters away until he gave up and left. Instead of taking a small step, it was easier just to run.

The pebble kept irritating until a short time later I was doing some cleaning around my flat to keep things neat and tidy. I saw a one-meter length of rope with a short piece of garden hose lying on a pile of grass clippings next to my landlord's garden shed. They were too short to be of any use realistically, and to me, this was a pile of rubbish. But I was so hard up that anything that was being thrown out was still precious to me. I did not like throwing anything out because things could always be reused in some way. I was certain that I would eventually find a use for them somewhere, somehow. I was ashamed to admit it, but someone's rubbish was like gold to me. I was on my way out for dinner, so I quickly put them in my car boot on my way out.

Later, I got home to find a note stuck to my door stating that my landlord had watched me "steal" those items and that they were not prepared to have a thief living under their roof, influencing their children. I was amazed. Those niggling issues had eventually surfaced as conflict over a small misunderstanding, as I saw it. There was no way that this could be ignored, swept under the carpet, and not acknowledged like other issues. So I went upstairs to straighten out this mix-up, but before I could open my mouth, I found that I had walked into a tirade. No longer was I simply confused and curious. I was actually troubled, and upset at how I had been greeted! Maybe it was a sudden release from suppressed emotions and pressure. Sound familiar? It was almost reminiscent of that storm years before when I left home, but with the roles reversed. I will never know. I must admit that once again, I reverted to what I had become comfortable with and ran from the conflict. I told him that I would be gone within two weeks.

As a result, another search began for a new place to lay my head. Thankfully, that weekend I had agreed to house-sit for a friend, so I could step out of the situation for the next few days at least. Once I began the new search intensively, I was introduced to an ambulance officer who lived a few suburbs away and rented a house on his own. I borrowed a utility truck and moved all my things over. Most things I could lift by myself, but as for an old battered fridge, I needed a second set of hands. Better than my word, I got everything moved over within one week. I had moved out with time to spare.

My new housemate and I got on well with each other. He did his shift work, and I had the house to myself. When I had first been left on my own in the granny flat, it seemed a bit too quiet and lonely, but I now found myself looking forward to that quiet and actually enjoyed the respite that it provided for both my study and emotional restoration. It allowed me times of undisturbed study as well as opportunities for reflection and rejuvenation. I was becoming more at peace in myself.

Simply moving to a new house did not remove the pebble though. There was still more to learn. This would come eventually, but one of the first lessons I would have to learn was to live within my physical abilities and limits. It would take a bit longer and a few more lessons.

9

Intermission

Interruptions are sometimes
God's way of saying, "Slow Down!"

After I left school, I became involved in Scripture Union Family Mission (SUFM) beach missions at Kingscliff, in northern New South Wales (NSW) for several years. I didn't realize it at the time, but this would be how my emotional rejuvenation would begin. When the director stepped down, the team asked me to take on the role. It had to be officially endorsed by SU Queensland, however, and after I sat down to be interviewed, I just waited for what I felt would be a simple case of dotting the I's and crossing the T's.

So, when I received a call to say that they would not be supporting my leadership and instead asked who I would recommend, I had to quickly pick myself up off the proverbial floor before I was able to respond. I was bemused and shocked at the same time. I wrote in my journal that night, "I feel like I'm about to enter the ring for another round with Satan. The reason given was the MS."

After that phone call, I rang the friend who I had recommended. I said, "I want you to go for it, and I'll support you in prayer and help you out in any way I can." I found it tough to accept that people thought that because I had a certain disease I was not useful in such a ministry as one in which I felt I had shown talent and gifting. I was beginning to get a small glimpse at the answer that God had for me. There were other ministries in which God could and would use me in the future. Something like a sidestep. Maybe God had other plans for me rather than dentistry also. It was at this time that I also began to learn about intercession.

On an Insight for Living (IFL) message about David and his time in the Cave of Abdulla, Chuck Swindoll made a point about regret that caught my attention and helped me put a new perspective on this news. It was a summary of what he had written in his book on David:

When the sovereign God brings us to nothing, it is to reroute our lives, not to end them. Human perspective says "Aha. You've lost this, you've lost that. You've caused this, you've caused that. You've ruined this, you've ruined that. End your life!" But God says, "No, no you're in the cave. But that doesn't mean it's curtains. That means it's time to reroute your life. Now's the time to start anew!"[10]

I began to see how God was answering my sincere prayer in eleventh grade to pull my life apart, rebuild it, and now reroute it. I was certainly finding that God can do anything, anytime, anywhere with anyone. He can use all circumstances for good, even those that we find bad. We cannot limit Him. He is too big. I too could say that I had lost this, I had caused that, and I had ruined both this and that. And yes, I even thought about ending my life at times. But in this moment, I began to accept that there had been a reason for it all. A reroute.

Looking back, I can say that I am thankful for that rejection to become a mission director because it is well known that there are three things that do not agree with MS—heat, physical exertion, and stress. And as director of a beach mission, all three things come with the territory!

Unknown to me at the time, opportunities would arise years later in ministry within the local church. Ministry at the right time. God's time! And in the same way, God was showing me that just as in ministry, dentistry was not the only thing I could do. My calling at the time was to focus on the small issues (i.e. study), but in the long term, I was being rerouted away from academia and dentistry.

As a result of this rejection, I found myself penning some words in my journal:

You're all I need
And Oh! I need You now
I know You can meet my need
I don't know how
You'll do it at the moment
But, You're all I need

Turn this around to "You're all *they* need," and you are starting down the path of intercession. The door had been closed to ministry on the Beach Mission stage, yet a window was being opened for me in the form of intercessory prayer. I would find shortly that indeed God goes before us to close doors preemptively and put the pieces in place for our very best before we even know it. Even when it does not make sense to us, His hand is still at work.

At the same time as this letdown was happening, I was asked to go to the Hillsong Conference scheduled for July that year (1994), which would fall six months prior to when the Beach Mission was to be run. I had been thinking that I would not be able to afford the time if I was to be preparing for the Beach Mission. But once this obstacle was removed, I was free to go. In time, I would see that God had closed the door to Beach Mission purposefully with what was around the corner. As always, He would be all I needed, and He knew best.

In July, I went down to the Hillsong Conference in Sydney. It was a great week focused on creative ministries. I learned a lot during daily workshops and was greatly encouraged during times of teaching and worship each evening. I saw a wide vista of how God can use those available to Him. Then on the second to last night, I went into an evening meeting and sat down. I was about to see God's preemptive working and the beginning of a reroute.

This night was no different from previous nights. I was looking forward to maybe hearing something that might impact my future while God continued to gently sculpt the direction of my life, just as He did one evening long ago back in that tiny granny flat (see "Run, Run, Run," chapter 5). As hoped, there was invigorating worship, inspiring teaching, and individual guidance. Dentistry was not the be all and end all in life; rather, a relationship with Him was the main thing. I would get impacted that night in a way that I had not foreseen.

At the end of the meeting, I went to stand up and found nothing happened. My brain said, "Shuffle the feet back, hands on the armrest, straighten the knees, take the weight, and stand up out of the chair." But there was no response. My head said one thing, but my body was not listening. I could do nothing but remain sitting in my chair. I was unable to stand and support my weight or walk, so I was carried out to a car and driven back to our host family, where I crashed onto a mattress on the floor for the night, hoping that after a good night's sleep, I would improve for the final day of the conference. I hoped that maybe it was just exhaustion, but the next day I was no better.

There was no way I could attend any sessions that day, so I literally dragged myself to a phone (I still could not walk) and rang an uncle in Sydney. On his advice, I headed to the nearest hospital emergency room. They sent me back to Brisbane on a plane (there was no way I could return home on a twenty-four-hour bus trip the same way I had traveled down to the conference). This turned out to be my first experience of a major MS relapse.

I was due to start my second semester in my fourth year of dentistry the following week. Years ago, I had been warned by the specialist who had confirmed my diagnosis that there was no future in this profession. And now, in my eyes at least, the end had come sooner than I expected. I could not walk, so I thought that this relapse was the end of any dream of studying or working in any paradental field either. Thinking to myself, *Well, that's the end of the line,* I withdrew from the dental degree completely.

I could not bring myself to let three and a half years' worth of dental studies go to waste. So, I decided to switch to a Bachelor of Dental Studies degree (an honors degree that could be done at any time after the third year of a dental degree had been completed) in forensic anthropology. Normally a twelve-month research degree, this ended up taking eighteen months before I submitted a thesis.

When I had been in first-year dentistry, we did a couple of oral biology subjects taken by a man who had been the consulting forensic dentist for the Queensland Police Force for nearly thirty years. He had sustained severe injuries when he was struck by a car a few years later, forcing him to retire prematurely. He offered to be an unofficial supervisor for my thesis. And with my other two official supervisors, I had a top line up of

- one of the top oral pathologists in Brisbane,
- the current consulting Queensland Police forensic osteologist,
- the former consulting Queensland Police forensic dentist.

My thesis consisted of recording the dentitions of pre-settlement indigenous Australian groups during a radiographic study. I ended up being able to graduate with a Bachelor of Dental Studies in the same ceremony along with my original dental classmates, which was very special for me. It was reinforcement that God could use previous effort despite current circumstances. Another lesson I had learned in my early years. Nothing goes to waste in God's economy.

Because I completed this degree in a part-time capacity, I was able to devote significant time to allowing God to sort my head out, something I would not have been able to devote myself to had I been studying dentistry full-time. And while I completed this research degree, I found that God continued to restore me, not just emotionally but physically as well. By the time I was nearing the completion of that degree, I began thinking and praying about my next steps. It had been a chance for God to show me that dentistry was not my only option. He used this as a circuit breaker, as I had been so focused on finishing dentistry that I needed something to break through that single-minded focus. This certainly did the job.

Eighteen months later, I had recovered enough after the relapse that I felt I could probably complete the dental degree so long as I paced myself (there was that never-give-up and never-let-go after something was started attitude once more), but on the other hand, I had a real interest in doing some Bible college. But where did God want me? I had no idea. I could see myself happily pursuing either path, but was God pointing me in a new direction? Was I being rerouted? For the first time, I was at least open to God leading me into His desired future rather than what I pictured as His plan for my life.

I had definitely been led into dentistry years before, but had I already achieved what God wanted by simply finishing a Bachelor of Dental Studies degree? Now, should I return to finish what I begun, or was there more? I decided to lay out a metaphorical fleece (à la Gideon in Judges 6) and reapply for entry back into fourth-year dentistry. If I was meant to continue in dentistry, I would be accepted; otherwise, I would take this as a sign that I was meant to go to Bible college. I sent a letter requesting reentry before sitting back to wait for God's answer.

There was no response, so I waited and waited, but there was no word. I still had a strong desire to pursue dentistry, but I just had to wait. Finally, the deadline for applications to Bible college came. I knew I would have to submit the college application forms by the due date.

If the silence continued, the door would be shut. I still could not shake seeing what God had done previously, so I delayed until the very day that applications closed and decided to wait for the post before I got in the car to drive over to a local Bible college to sign up. In the mail that day was a letter from the dental faculty office to say that I was successful in my application to reenter dentistry as a fourth-year part-time student. God had put me back into dentistry without any doubt or question! I was rejuvenated, and He had resurrected my original commission. The real question was, What would I do with this opportunity?

The answer had come that I should continue to pursue dentistry, regardless of whether or not I understood why. And I did not! I just knew that this was where God wanted me, so no matter what it took, I would do my part. Time for that tenacious pit bull spirit.

10

Relapses, Reroute, and Resolution

If you're at the end of your rope,
thank goodness God has a good catch.

And so, to make the study manageable (a four-year slog to complete the degree was too much all at once), I focused on the small things first. It became a case of one semester at a time. Like the saying about how to eat an elephant, I needed to break things down into one mouthful at a time, which meant that I needed to focus on finishing my degree one semester at a time as my number one priority. I found that I needed to pursue this at any cost, including my long-term health.

After I returned, it seemed that each year I would go into hospital with another relapse. It was never as severe as what I experienced down in Sydney but enough that I had to stop. A week's rest in the hospital, a course of IV prednisone (another corticosteroid to dampen inflammation), and I would be right to go again until the next year. I knew that this was draining my ultimate health status, but I was willing to pay this price even so since I knew that this was where God wanted me.

It became a race. Could I finish study before another major relapse, which would put a definite end to it all? There would be no coming back if another major relapse occurred, yet if I paced myself carefully, maybe I would be able to finish and head into research or academia if that was where I was led. In the final two weeks of doing practical work, I needed to strap one of my wrists for added strength and support to prolong my endurance during those final clinics. The finish line was approaching. Could I make it?

I am the kind of person who likes to achieve and to show that you can get somewhere and do things successfully. By nature, I push myself until the job is finished. And as shown by my resorting to strapping my wrist, I would keep going until I found a way to beat whatever I was struggling with. No matter what it is, no matter what the cost. It was a principle I learned and have operated on since early in my life—a principle obvious when I dug that drainage trench along the boundary fence, rode my bike across the city for work, or in my high school studies when I was told to simply give in. And now, I would carry this principle into my pursuit for a degree in dentistry.

With MS as a disease, I could not beat it; I could only live with it. It was that same concept of jumping off a bridge or learning to live with it. Those were the only two choices (as I thought), so I found it pretty tough because for the first time in my life, here was something that I could not beat or work around. I felt this way (which was quite depressing) until I realized that there was a third option. I could give it all to God and trust Him. And then I could watch Him use me and do some amazing things.

God had been repeatedly asking me to hand everything over to Him in the previous years. Even though I thought I had learned that lesson, as is natural, I found it harder to let go of the reins when the proverbial rubber hit the road. Instead of letting go, I kept pushing on in my own strength as I always had done, which was detrimental to me generally and to my health specifically. Put plainly, I struggled to learn the lesson to hand it over fully. It was not until those final weeks when I could only continue by strapping my wrist that I succumbed to this lesson and handed each clinic over to God. He gave me strength for each of those last clinics.

I did not expect God to take away my MS, but slowly I came to realize that He would always be on my side. And subsequently, if I kept my eyes fixed on Him, that would do two things:

a) It would be sufficient—because He would give me the strength I needed as I needed it, something He has done time and again.
b) It would help keep my eyes off the sidelines (including the past), things that would distract me and take my focus off my final goal.

Looking back, God used my time in research to teach and equip me for the task He had in store for me. His plans would become more focused with time.

Years earlier at a youth camp, on hearing a guest speaker by the name of Doris van Stone, I bought her autobiography, but as with many books,

I added it to my bookcase unread. After I returned to my dental studies, I picked it up and sat down to read it for some light reading. Again, I found that God had been preparing the way well in advance. Years later, I now found this book actually helped me crystalize who and what I was in God's sight. It also helped to better seat in my mind both where I was currently and what path He wanted for me in the future. It helped me come to terms with my MS and to hand the reins over to God.

What Doris had said mirrored some of my own thoughts. "I was scared. Maybe God didn't want me to be an artist after all. Art was my talent, my only profession. 'Lord, I can't do anything else', in the same way I told Him, hoping He'd be convinced … My commitment though sincere, was not seamlessly complete."[11] In the same way, I had been wrestling with God as to whether maybe He did not want me to be a dentist (an artist in her case) even though in my eyes it seemed like it was what suited me perfectly. I had originally thought I could do nothing else. Was God listening to me though? Over time, He had been slowly rebuilding my life one brick at a time and rerouting it.

As with Doris, my commitment had not yet been complete. I had given my life fully to God in tenth grade, but complete daily surrender would not come until a rural expedition (see next chapter). How did He want me to use my talents and gifts if I was not meant to remain in this arena? I was asking the Lord to show me what He wanted me to do instead of dentistry, even though as far as I was concerned, that was the only thing that I could do for Him. Could I convince Him? Or more importantly, was I prepared for the answer? As He said to Doris, "I'm not asking you to fill His [*Charles Diebler—a martyr*] shoes, but to walk in the same way" (italics added).[12] And once I had that answer, did I have the strength to see it through?

I had my doubts. Growing up, I used to look at great Christian identities and think, *They're the ones at the pinnacle of walking with God.* In my faulty thinking, they had discovered the secret to becoming acceptable to God. They were saints who I could never follow or be like. In my immature understanding, it was not just filling the shoes of Jesus; it was filling the shoes of these Christian greats. But there is nothing that we can do to add to the salvation that He offers, something I had not fully grasped.

Although I tried hard in my youth, it was to no avail, and I was doomed to fail time and time again because I had not been right with God. Like trying to put a small adhesive dressing strip over a broken leg, my attempted remedies never fixed the real problem. Eventually, I came to learn that all I needed to be and all that I was ever asked to be was 100 percent for Christ! To simply rest in the fact that God accepted me despite who I was, not *because* of who I was.

None of us can come to God in our own strength, capability, or identity because none of us are where we should be. We need to rest in the fact that we are accepted and then focus on the small things. In my case, this included affairs of this life—right then, study. That was how I needed to approach the completion of my degree. If God so desired, He could and would bring about the big items. All I needed to do was focus on the small issues. Sort of like David who was just busy looking after some sheep when a giant got in the way! I just needed to focus on where I was and what God had given me to do.

Focusing on the small things does not remove difficulties or hardships, but it certainly makes the big things more manageable and doable. This is what I resolved to do, to continue to push on and focus on the small things, leaving the big things to God and focusing on my job—studying. In her book, Doris recounts the testimony of a missionary named Darlene Diebler-Rose, who had been interred in a Japanese POW camp, and the fact that all she was able to focus on were those small things. But this would lead into bigger things down the track.

> After Pearl Harbor, Japanese troops had swarmed into the Dutch East Indies ... Then inexplicably ... Darlene's husband, Charles, was sent to a concentration camp, where he experienced brutality, rotten food, and disease ... Darlene ... did not learn of her husband's death until two months later. A fellow prisoner smuggled the news to her and gave her a pencil sketch of her husband's grave (a mound of dirt topped with a cross). She had lost everything. All her belongings were destroyed. Even their marriage certificate had been so badly charred in the bombings that it disintegrated ... "Young people," she said, "it cost me everything to serve the Lord." She paused, then added, "For Jesus' sake, I'd do it again."[13]

She became one of those Christian greats to me. I noted in my journal after reading this account, "I desire to have the same courage in my walk." She had lost everything yet displayed the courage to say, "I would do it again." This time, instead of being discouraged, I found it inspirational as I started to climb back up from my own pit of despair, where I felt that I too had lost everything. It was a lesson on keeping the main things the main thing (i.e. Christ). I was beginning to learn the lesson in my life that praise destroys despondency and dissipates depression.

By keeping my focus on the big picture and addressing the small issues, I felt like my life was starting to be restored. I learned to always praise God in all things and to look at the glass as being half-full rather than half-empty. This led to me focusing on what I could do rather than what I could not do, a philosophy I have since embraced as a life principle. Eventually, I too would be able to say, *If the same things were needed to give the same result, yes, I would do it all again.* And I can still say it today.

But before I came to this peace, there needed to be a rerouting of my life, which began just after I moved out of that granny flat in May 1994, when everything came to a grinding halt—walking, driving, studying, and ministry. Maybe one day I would learn why. But even if I did not learn it this side of heaven, I knew that this was what I needed to do—to walk in the same way and to focus on the here and now (the small things). My purpose was to complete a bachelor's degree in dentistry.

I continued my course of study, and slowly but surely, I chipped away step by step at the small things. It took four years to eventually graduate in November 1999. True, I never worked in the profession, research or academia, but I have a strong peace that this was where God wanted me.

So, when it came to my graduation ceremony, I thought, *If I am in a wheelchair, what other people think does not matter. I am receiving that piece of paper for what I achieved (past tense), and whether I walk up to receive it or whether I wheel in doesn't really matter. It is what I did previously (becoming a qualified dentist), not what I do now!* To finally graduate gave me great satisfaction, but I still did not know what direction God wanted me to take after all of this was said and done.

He was faithful, time after time, in helping me to cross the finish line of academic study, but that was not the only thing. He showed me that dentistry was not the only path (just as art was not the only path for Doris). And I have found that in the end, I can say with Darlene that I would do it all over again because I am in a much better place, with the promise of a much better place ultimately. Focusing on and striving to complete the dental degree was my way of giving some glory back to God for that faithfulness.

11

Bush Bash

God will still be at the
end of your highway!

It took several years to unravel that tangled ball of emotions, all the while chipping away at my study. Several things helped—time, talking things over with close friends, confidantes, and counsellors, listening to preaching on the Word of God, reading, and journaling. All of it helped in different ways to get my thoughts straight and resolve issues, while God at the same time softened my spirit, which allowed Him to restore and heal relationships. Things did not change overnight, but just like my study, that tangled mess was chipped away at, and it slowly improved. Sometimes the process was agonizingly slow and more akin to using a toy hammer to break up a granite mountain—slow but in this case needed.

Despite many lessons along the road of restoration and rerouting, one weekend in June 1996 was especially significant in helping me to clear my mind, get back on track with study, and gain a second breath in reconciliation, which at that particular time had seemed to slow to a crawl. In fact, the weekend started with me running and running until I not only reached the end of the street but then the end of the road, and finally, as Keith Green described it, I reached the end of my highway.[14] This was how the weekend started, but it became a time of seeking the Lord and hearing from Him in a very special way. He ministered to me, and I was restored before being reminded of how I stood before Him. As Doris van Stone put it:

> The cross of Christ is the perfect remedy for the entangled
> messes of human misery. Christ anticipated all the ugly
> things of life—he foreknew the birth of all mankind and

included everyone equally in His death. The question is whether they will respond to His love.[15]

In recent years, I had simply been existing, not living. I was miserable but knew no other reality, so my only response was to just keep pushing on.

Years before, God had reassured me, "You Are Mine." The question was, What would I do in response? The first thing I did following this revelation was to endeavor to trust God and follow Him wherever He wanted me to go. As much as my faith was imperfect at times, I knew that there was nothing else to do. At this time, that meant completing my dental degree. While I had been directly led to return to my studies, it was not always easy. The process had certainly been a journey in itself. It felt like I had been pushing in my study continually since my return, and as a result, I was close to exhaustion.

One Friday afternoon, I had what could be called a bad clinic at the Dental School. I had been doing a minor oral surgery (extraction) clinic when I found my arm fatigued rapidly on what should have been a simple extraction. Suddenly it became too much for me physically. I just did not have enough arm strength, so I called my demonstrator over to complete the procedure for me. With years of experience, he was able to whip the tooth out rapidly without any effort. I was so discouraged that I approached him after the clinic, to have him pose the question in no uncertain terms as to whether I should really be doing dentistry at all: "What's the point?"

I was confused. I had miraculously gained entry back into dentistry a few months earlier. And I knew that it had been God who had put me there. The why I did not know, but I knew from previous experience that He was never inconsistent with Himself. So would not reverse that direction now. But it seemed like I had been put back into this course only to find it too demanding physically. How was I supposed to fulfil my end of the bargain?

Looking back on it, God *did* put me back in that course, yes. But despite this fact, He never said that He would make it easy and hand it to me on a platter. It is a natural part of learning to struggle with a concept until you master it. And while you would think this would come naturally to me, considering my never-give-up attitude, sometimes even I would look for easier ways and shortcuts. At that time, I needed to learn the best technique so that minimal energy would be exerted in achieving my goal. And it was not my place to tell God how I wanted my lessons to come (easy or hard), just like a verse in Romans.

But who indeed are you, a human being, to argue with God? Will what is molded say to the one who molds it, "Why have you made me like this?" Has the potter no right over the clay, to make out of the same lump one object for special use and another for ordinary use?

(Rom 9:20–21 NRSV)

In general, I have learned to critically assess how I spend my time—special or ordinary. This extends across all aspects of my life because I cannot waste time or energy on things that do not matter. Critical assessment in daily living has become second nature to me. Another way of looking at it is that I am decisive in having a reason for everything that I choose to do, even when it may not make sense, usually because I have found that more efficient method for me. I cannot be doing things one particular way when there is a more efficient way to achieve the same outcome that saves energy. Since energy levels can be extremely low, with muscle contractions requiring large amounts of energy to lift very light objects (if at all—eventually, to even lift your arm becomes too much), it is important to find techniques to make the most of life. And to make every lift count. Sort of like the joke, "You know you're old when you bend down to tie your shoelaces and think, *What else can I do while I'm down here?*"

It may mean resting on the couch for the morning to save enough energy to go out in the evening or sheltering in air-conditioning while family are out on a hot day. These are the things I still find difficult. We have two growing boys who need physical outlets and a chance to experience life. I try to do as much as I can, but I have to accept that I cannot allow my limitations to dictate or hinder their activities. It becomes a case of doing as much as I can but not overdoing it. Back when I was studying though, I still had to put the hard yards in while learning to make my energy consumption as efficient as possible and saving it where I could. It was during these years of part-time study that I began to learn this lesson.

Stepping back to that bad clinic, I was demoralized. Sometimes I learned my lessons slowly and needed them repeated again and again.

I would later remember a lesson I had learned years before about glorifying God in whatever situation I found myself (including those that were difficult). I had learned this lesson when I had asked for healing and not received it (more about that later). But now, while what followed was not dishonoring as such, it was what I needed to do in my stage of emotional exhaustion. I found that God still works when we do not necessarily trust in and rely on Him.

After my discussion with that demonstrator, I left the Dental School well after everyone else had departed for the weekend, and as I walked down the hall across the air bridge connecting the two buildings, all I heard was the click of my shoes on the polished floors. My footsteps echoed down the deserted corridors while the persistent hum of the air-conditioning condenser created a low, incessant background drone. It sounded hollow, like my spirit, as I headed for home.

I was dejected, depressed, and despondent. I climbed into my car and drove home in silence, arriving after dark. The key slid into the lock, and there was a quiet click as the door was unlocked and swung open. I walked through the back door as my shoulders slumped with a heavy sigh. It had been a stressful week both at university and as far as family relations went. Things had been getting better with my family overall, but there were still occasions when tension rose. This week had been one such week. Reconciliation seemed to be going one step forward and two steps back at times before catching up with a slow step forward.

I felt that I was on the verge of breaking once more and had to just get away, so once again, I did what had become easiest and ran. As I walked through that door and put my things down, I knew exactly what I was going to do, just as when I started to climb that set of stairs when I left home so long ago. I loaded a pile of books, my Bible, some paper, a tarpaulin, and some food in the car. Then, within fifteen minutes, I was gone. I did not even leave a note for my housemate. I just drove.

On Friday night, I kept driving until I found myself on a secluded dead-end road near Noosa Heads. I tied the tarp onto the side of the car, laid out my sleeping bag, and spent a broken night's sleep shivering, shaking, and thinking, with a bit of prayer thrown in for good measure. Leaving around dawn, I kept driving like I was being pursued by some unseen force. Stopping only for petrol, I drove and drove through Saturday, praying and crying out to God while I drove.

At one point, I detoured from the highway and drove out along an unsealed logging road through the middle of a pine plantation/state forestry reserve (there are many of these dotting the countryside in this area). After twenty minutes of pushing my way deeper and deeper into the bush, I stopped in a clearing. I set up camp in the rain and thick mud, thinking I could settle down there for the day. The only sound that disturbed the stillness was the pitter patter of the rain falling on the tarpaulin tied up on one side to my car doors and pinned under rocks on the other.

A thought suddenly crossed my mind, and I began to fear that being in such a secluded location meant that if I got into difficulty, it could be weeks before anyone came along, especially since I had not told anyone of my plans. Was I courting danger? I was just asking for trouble if something went wrong. When the reality of this situation sank in, I quickly packed up and found my way back along the bush tracks (which were little more than sodden clay paths) to the highway. On some hills, the tires should not have gained traction. I believe some supernatural help was involved. Thankfully, the route that I had traveled came back to me, and as the rubber hit asphalt, I whispered a prayer of thanks that there had been no incidents, and I drove on.

Heading into the hinterland, I kept going until eventually I pulled over beside an embankment covered with nearly two-meter-high razor grass and turned the engine off. Since the night before, as well as writing in my journal, I had progressively been writing a list of all my struggles, recurring sins that I fought against, and all that was wrong in my life on a piece of paper. Basically, I had been running and running since leaving home years before, until I had reached my breaking point that previous night. I had been driving and driving ever since, until now when I reached the end of my highway, as alluded to by Keith Green in his song, "Run to the End of the Highway."[16]

Now, I sat slumped over the steering wheel, confessing, repenting, crying out for God's forgiveness, touch, and help in each of these areas longing to be restored. I sat with my eyes closed, tears pouring down my cheeks while the rain fell consistently on the roof of the car. I heard the rain ease off a little and took the opportunity in a symbolic act to crumple up that piece of paper, step out of the car, and throw it as far as I could while I screamed at the top of my lungs, *Satan, be gone! I am not yours! I have been purchased by the blood of Jesus. He is mine, and I am His!* It was reminiscent of a scene in the movie War Room where one of the main characters, Elizabeth Jordan, chases Satan out of her house and life, reclaiming it as God's ground. This movie was released years later, but I had a strange sense of déjà vu when I finally watched this scene.

Before this point, I thought that so long as I did certain things and did not do others, I would be a successful Christian. As a result, I would fall into the trap of questioning whether or not I was actually saved. Satan had a field day making me doubt the validity of my salvation. And although I had been saved in my youth and I would make a profession of faith, try really hard, but then fall back on my old way, it was not until I did a total about-face in my life in tenth grade that the importance of a daily walk emerged in a new way to me.

The fact that my efforts and living up to expectations (even though they were my own) could never make me more acceptable to Him had become even more real. Whatever I did was ordinary compared with everyone else. No longer did I need those achievements to make myself secure. I was no longer insecure. My status was now found in Jesus, not me. I made the decision to continue my journey of discipleship with Jesus each and every day.

There were still many things that hampered me from running my race well. Before this point in the hinterland, I had only known Jesus as my savior, not as Lord and King. I neglected Jesus for years after I asked Him into my life. Despite becoming a fully committed follower in tenth grade, I still had not fully internalized that gift, so how could I expect to be protected from the inevitable attacks of Satan? Now, God was getting at the root of my fallen human nature. I had learned that I needed to submit daily to the Lordship of God. It was on this roadside that I made Jesus not just my savior but Lord as well! It was all part of my long marathon (the long journey of obedience, as some refer to it) to put Christ at the helm.

And now, enough was enough. I realized that my salvation had been sealed many years ago. The issue was my daily growth and walk as a Christian. As Paul put it in the letter to the Colossians (Col 2:20–22), it is not a matter of not doing a list of things (and following a set of human rules), it is having a personal relationship with Jesus Christ ("dying to the elemental spiritual forces of this world").

Sometimes we accept the free gift on offer from God and receive salvation (that moment when all that is wrong in our lives is imparted/ put on Jesus's shoulders, and we are given His righteousness/purity in its place, what is known as justification). But it is the process of sanctification (being purified and becoming more like Jesus) that becomes the battlefront where Satan does his best to sabotage our faith. We start off our spiritual journey being clean, but it is amazing how easy it is for the waters to become murky once more, and we need to be cleaned up again. And if he gets an opportunity, Satan will ask the question, "Are you sure you are good enough to receive salvation?" This had been my experience. On my invitation, my life had been pulled apart by God, and the residual issues that caused those murky waters were cleaned up. It allowed Him to take full control of my life, as my old self was replaced with a new nature. As in 2 Peter 1:4, it was not just a case of me being cleansed once when I received my salvation; it was a process of ongoing sanctification performed step by step. It was the reason one obstacle after another had been progressively removed from my life, leaving a bare plot of land that could be replanted.

To cultivate the soil in one's life so that God can do what He wants, sometimes He needs to clean out obstacles and debris. I have also heard it described as being a boulder of recurrent sin, a weed of rebellion, or a stump of disobedience. So, in some instances, He needs to use a weed whacker/slasher to clean out the plot, and sometimes He needs to do some major work and use some dynamite. Depending on what the core problem is, the tools differ. It is all a case of the right tool for the right job. At times, God had to resort to dynamite to remove obstacles and prepare the soil of my life for Him to do what He wanted with the rebuilding phase.

Another way of looking at it is presented by Jeremiah as he observed the potter at work and pointed out that God (as He is entitled to) decided that the vase (my life) was not what He wanted, so following my invitation, He (the potter) discarded it and then shaped the lump of clay into something else, "shaping it as seemed best to Him" (Jer 18:4), and it was not exactly comfortable! But this whole process had been the beginning of when my identity was to be found in Jesus. And now, for the first time, I fully accepted the grace of God and submitted to His Lordship, which alone made me acceptable.

There is nothing we can do to live the Christian life and make ourselves acceptable or more loved, and there is nothing that can make Him love us less. It was only on this revelation that I fully put my life into His hands, and it was only at this point that it began to be built into a dwelling that both God and I would be happy to live in. He began to rebuild it brick by brick. I needed to allow this reshaping by the potter (in terms of a vase) and accept that grace wholly, absolutely, and without reserve. Yet it still took a while for me to stop paddling in my own strength. Sometimes it takes a while to get rid of the weeds and garbage that clutter up the garden. But this led to another major step in my growth in Christ.

What was the difference now though? Did I suddenly become worthy? No! On my invitation, He had broken me down to my foundation in order to take me further. Remember, there is nothing we can do to make ourselves acceptable. Instead, God was gracious to me yet again. It was a matter of grace that brought me to originally receive the gift of salvation as a child, and a matter of grace when I became fully committed in tenth grade. Once more, it was grace that continued my growth on the next leg of my marathon.

Once my identity was found in Jesus, whatever circumstances or condition I found myself in, I would have real peace because I knew that I was in the right race and running it in His strength, and that was okay! I had committed my life fully to God in tenth grade, but it was not until this rural expedition on being broken down that I learned and embraced the reality of His gift of grace to me, surrendering and handing Him absolutely everything and submitting myself to Him. Once this truth became real, the do's and don'ts simply fell into place. I found that although the road may have been unclear at times, the last command had not changed. And as is said in the military, "Always follow your last command." Dentistry was where I should be.

Likewise, it may be crucial when we begin both our physical and our spiritual life, but what is critical is how we finish our spiritual life, our relationship with God, and our race. We all can start the race, but it is important how we run the race and even more important how we finish it (Heb 12:1; 1 Cor 9:24; Gal 2; 2 Tim 4:7). After that major step, it would only be up the mountain from there.

Now that identity issues were resolved, I continued on and found myself at Lake Cootharaba (northwest of Noosa) where I set up camp once more. That night, I woke in the middle of the night and under the light of a full moon wandered down to the shoreline with a fresh piece of paper. I poured my heart out in writing as I sat contemplating where my life had ended up while soaking in my surroundings. It seemed to me that God had been at a distance, like a distant light on the other side of a great expanse of water, or a star high in the heavens. Clouds swept by to mask His presence. But I found that now, similar to when I had attempted suicide years before, I once more lectured myself with the truths that I knew in my head. While it seemed that God was distant and I could not see Him around me in my life, He was still present. And as I looked carefully, I saw glimpses between the clouds. Once more, I found that my best thinking was done as I wrote, and in the end, I had penned some words in the stillness while the water lapped gently on the sand at my feet. I later named those words, "I sit, I stand" (see appendix 2), and it was not until years later that I was reminded of how in this piece I was asking the same questions as David in his opening lines of Psalm 10, "Why, Lord, do you stand far off? Why do you hide yourself in times of trouble?" (Psa 10:1).

After emptying my heart out to God, I returned to my makeshift campsite and fell into a peaceful sleep. When I woke in the predawn of the next morning, my attitude had entirely changed. I packed up in the clear morning light and departed once more (but this time, it was not to escape something unseen). The rest of that weekend was a time of healing and personal restoration. I knew that I had been forgiven, restored, and recommissioned. God's rushing wind had fully blown through the temple of my life and cleaned it out. Following my salvation, this was the most groundbreaking event in my life. His grace had blown my fear away, so despite God's greatness being all around me, I just wanted to drive and explore it for myself. A weight had been lifted from my shoulders, and I felt free. I wanted to discover what was around the next corner, and the next, and the next …

I continued to drive and eventually found myself at Rainbow Beach, where I took a long walk to a popular tourist spot known as The Colored Sands—large sand hills pigmented in various vivid colors due to metallic residue in the grains of sand (ranging from yellow to black, green to white, and many colors in between). There I sat on the beach in front of an enormous sand hill, which was brighter than a vibrant oil painting, to pen the second half of the piece I had begun the night before. It was the reply to my heart's cry. I titled it "I Sit in Awe" (see appendix 3).

At about 4:30 p.m., knowing I had to report at the university the next morning for a clinic, I decided to head back to the car and start the long trip home. A few kilometers out of Rainbow Beach, I saw a sign for Brisbane that said 350 km. Knowing that by sealed roads I had traveled that weekend over double this distance, I believed I had at least a three to four hours of constant driving ahead of me.

I was still feeling adventurous and thought I would continue my exploits. I turned my little Toyota Coupe onto the unsealed road but got all of 700 meters before stalling the engine in a washed-out creek crossing in about one meter of water. I came to a grinding halt as the engine flooded. I had overestimated the capability of my little two-wheel drive car out in the bush. A Toyota Hilux it was not! In the same way with my MS, I needed to learn how to live within my physical capabilities. Ultimately, it was a lesson that I did learn, but God had to get me out of a few tight spots on the way. He was gracious!

I quickly wound down the window and climbed out so as not to let water flood in when the door was opened. And then I walked back to the main road in the hope of flagging a passing car down. But being dusk on a Sunday evening, the road was deserted. After waiting for a few minutes and seeing no passing cars, I headed back to my car to find that, as I had feared, water had started seeping in through the floor. While driving that weekend, the undercarriage of the car had taken a significant beating on the unsealed roads (at one point, even the stone guard under the engine had even fallen off). I hate to think what damage had been sustained. During this time, all of the books that I had grabbed on Friday night had been placed on the floor of the passenger foot bay. This would soon be underwater if the car was not moved, so I quickly climbed back in through the open window to transfer them all up onto the seat and buy some extra time before they all became nothing more than a mass of waterlogged wood pulp and ink. I resigned myself to the fact that I needed to somehow get the car out of the creek—and soon!

After taking my seat and buckling up, I prayed that God would in some way help. Why, I don't know, but there was not much else to do. Isn't it interesting that when we are totally out of options, only then will we turn to prayer! When we encounter problems, the first thing we should do is take it to God. But so often, it is the last thing we do. Well, God was still gracious. I paused, turned the key, and when I did, the engine spluttered to life while the tires gained traction. As I gently depressed the accelerator, the car slowly but steadily reversed on this one-chance-only attempt to get back up on firm ground. The car emerged, and I thanked God in glee and excitement for His supernatural intervention and His immediate answer to my prayer!

I headed back to the main road, turned left, and this time opted for the longer route home. I arrived home four hours later at 8:30 p.m., ready to face more high-pressure clinics and life in whatever form it took, knowing that God was with me and for me, even if I could not see Him directly. And most importantly, I knew where I stood. I had found my identity at the end of the highway. That weekend, I drove as far as Tin Can Bay/Rainbow Beach, three hours north. I drove as far as Kingaroy, two hours inland. As I drove, the car got a workout like never before, covering over 800 km. I had made the occasional campfire to toast bread to go with my tins of cold baked beans and spaghetti. I slept under a tarp on bare ground down remote side roads and in secluded camp grounds. I read my Bible, wrote in my journal, and read books. But I had never been able to concentrate long enough to get very far in any one of them. It had been a time when I could consciously deconstruct my thought patterns, and during that Bush Bash, the Savior became everything to me! I not only submitted but also surrendered all to Him.

Years ago, I felt that I had lost everything. But at the end of it all, I still had God, and my faith was stronger. Doris van Stone put it this way: "When you have nothing left but God, [*you*] realize that God is enough" (italics added).[17] It was not until this bush excursion that I fully came to terms with the lesson that God *was* enough. I was beginning to prove that God *is* enough as well.

It was at this time that the thought began to take shape in my mind that maybe, just maybe, my experiences and journey with MS may be used by God to build others up while encouraging them of His immense love and care for His children. I was beginning to see how God might be able to use my story in the midst of my disability and broken dreams. Doris van Stone observed, "One aching heart knows when another heart is aching ... [*And this*] enables me to say to others 'I know how you feel'" (italics added).[18]

On returning to the busyness of university life, I needed to perfect how to conserve energy and pace myself. That meant I needed to become content and be thankful simply to pass academically. And with more mature thought, it was a principle that I had observed and learned in my younger years from my father as we built furniture together. If there was a small imperfection in an item when we finished (e.g. a small dent in a piece of timber), he would say, "A blind man would be glad to see it!" It never meant much to me before my return to university, but it was to take on a whole new significance from this time on. To pass a subject by just scraping through may not have been what was originally planned, but now it was as significant as passing it comfortably. In the grand scheme of things, I had so much more to worry about in life; academic achievement and excellence were no longer as high on my list of priorities. So I could be truly thankful for any passing results. Basically, a blind man *would* be glad to see it. My expectations and perspectives were slowly coming into alignment. Now, my experiences, the turmoil that I had gone through, and my MS all enable me to say the same thing as Doris van Stone and give empathy to others when I have the chance.

Shortly after I received my diagnosis, I began to record my thoughts, emotions, and feelings not only in my journal but also in the form of songs. Over this period of three to four years, I found a new outlet for my emotions to be processed and my thoughts to be recorded while God counselled me. And in so doing, I found a way to share with others. Usually, they were without musical scores since I was not competent in composition. However, there were a few that a friend put to music. One such piece expressed my desire to share with an imaginary friend the plea to "take hold" of the gift of grace, but subconsciously it also revealed my new outlook to do what I could do while I could do it—to take hold of the moment now! (See "Take Hold," appendix 4.)

My writing during that weekend continued as I traveled across the countryside in southeast Queensland, and I documented my heart's cry. Years before, it had been a prayer that I uttered in response to a song, and that weekend it became a piece of poetic prose recording what I knew to be true regardless of what I felt. I was able to do dealings with God, let Him work in my heart, and process my emotions. This would inevitably lead to my reflecting on family relations so that these could, in turn, be dealt with.

The journey would continue slowly but purposefully on my return to the humdrum of life and study. My head was in a much better place, so I was able to cope with daily pressures and found my course of study back on track. I was able to handle the pressures so well that I was able to begin looking back and process where I had come from and what had happened in my life over the previous years. Part of that involved looking back through old journals. One day I was looking through some rough scribblings from my high school days when I stumbled across something I had written after listening to the song "Rushing Wind" by Keith Green. I had since forgotten about this incident, but as I sat reading those faded notes, I recalled vividly the heartfelt prayer I made to God that afternoon back in grade eleven. I sat speechless as I thought about how He had responded to my prayer for a rushing wind. He broke me and everything in me.

During training sessions in preparation for a Franklin Graham crusade years later, we were told how God could take us and use us so long as we simply made ourselves available to Him. In fact, He may just surprise us. Now at this point, following a confirmed diagnosis, my thought had been, *Yes, He certainly surprised me in the years following my prayer!* I never would have imagined what was before me and what turns my life would take in the years ahead—turns that would take me down some dark alleys but paths I would never resent.

After this period of being restored and rerouted, and the weekend of being reestablished and recommissioned, one more issue needed to be addressed.

12

Family

After a storm comes a calm.
—Matthew Henry

This was a very hard chapter to write since in years gone by, my family relationships were under extreme pressure before, when, and after I left home. There were things said and done that we all regret, but we have patched things up, rectified issues, and moved on as God brought about reconciliation, restoration, and healing. And through it all, He was faithful in not letting us go.

My sister was married before moving overseas just prior to when things exploded, so she was essentially isolated from being exposed fully to what happened. My parents and brother, unfortunately, were subjected to the entire journey. The road of reconciliation was full of not just mountains and valleys but also many potholes. It was painful, but slowly and surely, things improved. When I was feeling particularly disconnected from my family, it resulted in some of the heartaches outlined in earlier chapters. But as the saying goes, onward and upward. Then why, you may ask, dredge up the past? It is part of how I became who I am—how my outlook on life came into focus and how I tend to relate to people and circumstances. Rather than simply dredging up the past, it shows just how faithful God has been in my life.

When I started to look back, to resolve and deal with that ball of tangled emotions, I found that I had hurts from my parents' reaction to (as I saw it) my growing sense of independence but also from other family relations during that family breakdown, and this was made worse by the way I had learned to handle conflict as I grew up. The methods I had learned to use in my younger life became habitual and were to be repeated in later years in other interpersonal relationships, such as my first landlord and ex-girlfriend. They would be repeated because I just had not learned.

If I was to not be permanently hamstrung in my life, I had to let go of past pain and be willing to move on. Again, I found Doris van Stone put it in a way that resonated with me: "Reality crashed upon me like a huge breaker. As much as I would have liked to, I could not change the past. The Lord had a future for me I knew, but I could only go forward if I could let go of the past."[19]

While I never experienced the same degree of suffering as Doris, if I was to move forward with my life, I needed to let go of the past. Then and only then could I move on to the future that God had for me. Or another way of putting it was that if I let bitterness and resentment take hold, any chance of happiness would evaporate, and I would never be happy or have personal peace. This reality became significant and eventually helped me to step down from any high ground that I may have felt and seek reconciliation with my family.

However, before I could bring myself to step down, I went through a stage when even simple contact with my family would proliferate problems experienced in the past. The hurts continued to arise and buffet me, just like a series of dumpers at the beach. My emotions were not only tangled; they were raw, and any small abrasion became a cut that sliced and was felt deep. The greatest destructive event in anyone's life and the most difficult of circumstances to repair is the breakdown of family relationships—those closest to you and who know you best. Even though I had been a hypocrite in my earlier years, these were the people who would matter in the end. I found God sustained, guided, and promoted eventual reconciliation in the midst of all this chaos.

Even though I did not understand how, it was at the time when I was trying to juggle university study as well as life in general, including singleness and disability, that I found God opening my eyes to keep me going emotionally and psychologically. At times, I could not see my hand in front of my face, yet God was still doing work in my heart and in the hearts of my family, such that the hurts became less and less frequent, and together there was shared growth, and we began to smooth over and recover from the past.

Some issues took significantly more time to deal with. One example was a letter received from a relative a week after I left home. I was staying at my pastor's residence at the time, and it was handed to me as I rushed out the door one morning.

Unable to read it until I got to my then girlfriend's house, where I received a lift to the university each day, I sat on their study floor and got halfway through the first page before I broke down and just wept. With numerous censures and the hope for "failure out in the big world," there were many other tough things to hear coming from a relative, someone of my own blood. I never did finish it that day.

When I broke down, on realizing how fragile I was, my girlfriend's mother advised me to "put it in a box in your mind and leave it there until you are ready to deal with it." A day or so later, only by having it read to me was I able to finish it before putting it away in that mental box.

It would be nearly eighteen months before I was emotionally ready to take it out of that box and deal with it. I came to realize that I was holding onto this letter, which constantly reminded me of past hurts and so hindered any chance of reconciliation. Even with an eventual apology, I was cynical about any sincerity. And so, ever since receiving it, I harbored bitterness deep down. As a result, I constantly battled with depression. I knew that if I was going to move forward into the future, I needed to move beyond the hurts of the past.

I had been praying for quite some time that God would help me move beyond and put to rest any feelings that had erupted due to communications over the last couple of years, including this particular letter. And so one day I asked an uncle to sit down with me to discuss it. I was able to share my heart, aiming to put into words both history and current emotions, trying to understand why I was where I was. This time of confession, honesty, and discussion helped untangle this part of that ball of emotions and put to rest part of the bigger picture. He did not need to read the letter to discuss it, nor did he want to. After talking over the issues, we joined in a prayer of affirmation, after which I did not want it to remain in my possession any longer, as I knew it would poison me as long as it was in my hands. I left it with him to destroy. It was an opportunity to put into practice a lesson in keeping short accounts, although it had taken eighteen months to do so. As time passed, I realized that instead of holding on to things, I needed to let go and move on (with God's help if necessary).

I began to learn this lesson at this point, but did not fully grasp the concept until after I was married. This is coming a little bit ahead of the story itself, but for convenience sake, it can be discussed here. We are told in the letter to the Ephesians to "not let the sun go down while you are still angry" (Eph 4:26b). I learned a good principle, that this does not mean that you should not go to bed without issues of disagreement. Rather, to not go to bed with anger. If you do not agree and cannot find middle ground, agree to disagree until it is possible to revisit the issue under calmer circumstances the next day. Be sure not to sweep it under the carpet (my default position), but actually revisit it as agreed. And, before you retire, make sure that you reiterate and vocalise the importance and sanctity of your marriage vows. It took time, but eventually, I improved in living by this precept.

In my past, there had not been much success at this, but one thing I learned in married life was that I needed to keep short accounts. A disagreement may occur, but the issue could then be straightened out, apologies made, forgiveness given if needed, without keeping a record to be dredged up months later by saying, "You always do this. Remember when …" I certainly did not begin to master this until operating as part of a yoked couple. It is an ongoing process which hopefully will not come to an end until that final separation of death.

And this is why satisfaction levels for long-term married couples (fifty-plus years) are actually greater than those of newlyweds. They grow closer as one over time, always leaving room for improvement. The principle of short accounts was a lesson needed for true family reconciliation to occur. But regardless of the arena, it has been a lesson that has stood me in good stead ever since.

Another lesson learned was to grow a thicker skin and not to take everything to heart. I found that it was not necessarily what was said as how it was said (or how I perceived it to have been said) that could get my back up. There were times when communications came (mainly in the form of letters, videos/tapes, and books) that were gentle corrections or material that would help me in my spiritual growth and maturity, but from my point of view, they were expressions of disapproval or disappointment (there was that whole perception issue once more).

These were times when my emotions were sensitive to begin with, and I became suspicious of any apologies. My perceptions of normal conflict resolution became tainted. I felt that in the past, anything could be done or said before a simple sorry was given. And then it was expected that you should accept that apology before things moved on, ready or not! As for me though, this did not work. I was more likely to dwell on things rather than let them go. And in the past, I did not allow myself to accept an apology at face value and let go.

Many times, I took it the wrong way, and my anger was masked (something I had become proficient at), but at least I had begun to vent in my journal. At these times, I would vent while the Holy Spirit would counsel me. A release valve had been developed to prevent progressive pressure buildup once more.

Sometimes He was able to guide and counsel. But sometimes He had to pull me back from the brink. I was just too worked up, and it could take a few days before I fully cooled down. On one such occasion, I wrote in my journal, "I'm getting pretty close to just saying, 'Get out of my life and leave me be!' but so many people have expectations of me to be tolerant and loving etc.—I can only take so much!"

At these times, despite feeling pushed to my limits, I would eventually come around and accept that His way was best. There was also the reality of knowing that my personal testimony would be shot to pieces if I followed these emotional leanings to their ultimate terminal point.

While I was venting, I was in my own way talking and praying to God. It is a good thing that He has broad shoulders and we can share anything with Him in total honesty. We can share our secret feelings, our deepest hurts, and darkest fears. We can vent our frustrations, and He will not be angry or disappointed in us.

Instead, He will gently steer us in the direction that is best for us. I knew what I should do despite my hyperbole and threats, but I still found it ever so hard at times to do it. It was a slow and gentle journey to reconciliation—too slow at times.

It was then that my father stepped in. I credit him with taking the bull by the horns when he took me over to New Zealand for a ten-day touring holiday. I was still suspicious and gun-shy, so I went on the proviso that I held on to my return airfare ticket. He graciously agreed to this, and we were able to begin the process of informal reconciliation between the two of us.

After that trip to New Zealand, my studies and family reconciliation continued with renewed vitality. I sat my next set of exams, and following them, I came across a note I had written in my journal shortly after I had become single years before, after my diagnosis. The note prophetically put my feelings into words. I had written, "I still feel unsteady. Sort of like a baby who has just started walking. You can see that they can do it, but the confidence is not there. Maybe that'll come. Only God knows, right?"

Final reconciliation did not come until after my marriage, but for the sake of giving the full story, I will deal with it here. True to form, slowly but surely, God had given me that confidence in my studies. And now confidence also began to return to family relationships as they were restored.

I was beginning to apply my need to forgive and move on and do what I should do regardless. It took almost ten years to complete my university studies, but at the same time, it ended up taking nearly ten years for full family restoration. It may be considered as a season of wasted years, but on the other hand, my life was deconstructed in the end, and a better overall family unit came into focus along with that rebuilt life.

Wider family reconciliation continued slowly until after I was married and had finished study. Then I heard an Insight for Living (IFL) podcast on regret. While family reconciliation had been a slow process and still had not finished, I came to realize that my health could one day deteriorate to the point of being unable to express myself verbally. And this would lead to regret on all sides if things were not put right within my family. Not just regret, but it would lead to inevitable wasted years as well.

I came across some other words that I had scribbled on some lecture notes: "Bitterness will only contaminate me." I had later written in my journal, "Those words ring true because of a lot of things that life seems to have dealt me … Really, there is a lot that I can be bitter about and dwell on, but what's the use/point? It will only damage me!" This became part of the thought process which led me to seek reconciliation with my family. Again, God was faithful. He had been working in my mind to process all that had happened in my life. And when the opportunity arose, He gave me courage and strength to take the necessary steps.

Over the coming months, I looked for an opportunity to raise the past with my parents (the rest of those involved came later). I prayed and finally realized that it was time to stop praying and take action. It was time to broach the issue with them. After sitting them down one day, I simply stated, "I want to give an unreserved apology for sixteen years ago and subsequent years because there were things I did that I shouldn't have done. There were things I said that I shouldn't have said. And there were thoughts I had that I shouldn't have had. Basically, I want to say I'm sorry." It was a time of reconciliation; things were put right, and a huge weight was lifted from my shoulders.

Finally, I was emotionally ready and had processed that tangled ball of emotions. I sat my parents down and humbly sought forgiveness, final reconciliation, and restoration. Things were put right, bridges were completed from both sides, and horizons were opened up, allowing us to move forward.

I said to my wife that night after reconciliation had taken place, if my life was metaphorically like a house, this was the first time I felt like my house was in order. Or another way of looking at it was that the demolition phase was complete. Reconciliation had ensued. Purpose and redemption had been restored to my life, and it was well on the way to being rebuilt according to God's plan.

In a way, the words of one of my songs ("Take Hold," appendix 4), apart from being a plea for a non-Christian friend, also reflected deep feelings that I had during my journey of personal healing, and this would become relevant in the journey of seeking reconciliation. I needed to "take hold of the moment—now." Faltering steps were better than no steps at all. If ignored for too long, the chance could be lost forever. I needed to take them before it was too late. Today was the day! And this prompted me on to further action.

I did not recognize the significance of this need for action until years later. Its importance became evident when my father was diagnosed with a cancerous polyp in his bowel. He had it surgically removed, and chemotherapy was initiated to be absolutely certain of its treatment. He experienced septic shock and spent several days in ICU as a critical patient on the edge of life. The chemotherapy was ceased since it was only regarded as being a secondary line of defense. It was felt at the time that it was not really necessary.

Then in January 2016, they found advanced metastatic cancer. That last month, things were shared and bridges fully repaired, such that on the evening prior to his death, I was able to leave the hospital and sum things up to my wife as we drove out of the hospital car park that night by simply saying, "No regrets!" They were things that could not have occurred without full reconciliation.

He died on February 15, 2016, after what I call, 'a good month'! I never made it back up to the hospital in time for those final moments of his life on this planet, but we had said and communicated what we needed so that there were no regrets. In the end, it was not me who was unable to speak. If it had been left too long to say what needed to be said, it definitely would have been too late. But thankfully, things had been put right.

As a family, we had been through a phase when we were estranged. My parents did the best they could at the time. Yes, mistakes may have been made on all sides, but if it had not been for the godly leadership of my father, things may have turned out very differently. The loss of those we love is felt deepest when their contribution to our life is most significant. And the period of family breakdown was one that was not just significant for me, it was life changing. But as I once more stand on my own two feet, I look back and am thankful for my godly heritage and upbringing.

Salvation and faith are not two separate things. An integral part of salvation is putting one's trust in Christ. But it is not just down to us putting our trust in Him. Salvation in its totality is God's gift of grace to us. The fact that we have faith is likewise a gift from Him. It is something we must perceive to be able to accept God's offer and that produces salvation. Another aspect of this comes with the gifts of the Spirit, one of which is faithfulness. A gift and a fruit—a mystery. Likewise, touching on the mystery of predestination and free will, how is it that we could not believe before, but now we do? It is purely God's gift to us. But will we accept them—faith then salvation? And it was my godly heritage that laid a firm foundation for my faith, which would eventually lead to my salvation. It was something I did not fully appreciate until that final month of my father's life.

There is a verse in scripture that is often misrepresented; 2 Peter 3:8 closes with the words, "With the Lord ... a thousand years are like a day." The point of this verse is that there is no such thing as time in heaven because just before this, we are also told that "a day is like a thousand years" (2 Pet 3:8b). In reality, God and spiritual realms are entirely outside our time dimension. But if we were to apply the latter part of this verse in a way that we can relate to, it could be said that it works out that one hour (with the Lord) is like 41.666 years (earth time). So, I jokingly said at his funeral, "See you within the hour!" But somehow, I do not think I'll be around in forty-two years. Reunion will be sweet.

I had apologized and said sorry for any part I had played in past family turmoil. But we are told that we must forgive as well. To draw a line under the past, I needed to forgive anything that was done or not done, either real or perceived. It was not until this that I was able to say, "The past is gone. There is only the future. Let's make it count!" We successfully did that over those final years of his life.

Looking back, God did take my prayer for a rushing wind seriously and then pulled my life to pieces with a bit of dynamite where needed! I had grown up trying my best to be a good Christian and live up to the teachings of Jesus, but no matter how hard I tried, I just could not do it in my own strength. It was not until I gave God an open invitation to clean out everything that was wrong with my life that He took me up on my invitation and said, "Yes," accepting at my word. And it was not until I handed it all over to Him to live my life as He wanted that my life began to be built into a dwelling that both He and I were happy to live in.

And my goodness did that process hurt! But then, what else can be expected when a chisel is used on our lives to shape them? I had needed something more than a chisel, more like dynamite to remove obstacles in my life, and it was only then that the land was level and clear, allowing Him to begin to rebuild my broken life His way, brick by brick. Indeed, He was faithful and gracious to re-mold and reform the lump of clay in order to rework the piece of artwork/vase rather than just discarding it. I have heard it asked, "Do you want to live?" And my answer would be, "Yes, but right now I want to live my life His way!"

The Big Wait

Be patient.
God is writing your love story.
—Anonymous

A marvelous illustration of God's faithfulness happened when I was single and living on my own. I had a deep longing to have someone by my side to share myself with. Kenny Marks sums it up well in his song "Single Minded Love" when he speaks of the struggle between the desire to be "single and free and the desire to be coupled."[20]

I know that some people are meant to remain single, and I believe that singleness is a gift, not a burden (although sometimes there may still be a deep longing that comes with the territory). God somehow gives *extra* grace to meet the needs of people wanting that life companion when they are in fact meant to remain single. I cannot explain it, but in those circumstances, truly, His grace *is* sufficient. And it is possible to be a whole person living life to the fullest while being single. Being single does not make one a second-class person. These people are just as important and relevant and contribute to God's economy. This chapter is about how God provided for my needs and faithfully granted the cry of my heart while I got on with my life as a single person. It is also about looking back and seeing God's hand as He brought all the pieces together.

I had prayed numerous times, asking the Lord to be my sufficiency and to give me peace in any state that I might find myself, be it single or as part of a couple. One night, however, things felt different. As my heart's desires rose within me yet again, I found Satan started to manipulate those feelings and pressure those weaknesses that had characterized my earlier struggles from years gone by, turning them into thoughts that were neither wholesome nor spiritually healthy. I recognized quickly what he was doing and called out to the Lord to deliver me and again be my sufficiency.

Once more, He was faithful and met my plea and reassured me that His plan for me was perfect. But for now, I was called to be single. In time, it would all become clear. In the meantime, I needed to wait and keep my mind focused on that which was healthy and edifying. It is not a sin to be tempted, only to follow those temptations to the end point. And so, I found that I needed to ensure my mind was not left empty, bored, or directionless and at the same time turn my mind to things that were uplifting spiritually. Some people have found physical exercise useful. But in my situation where energy levels were a premium and physical activity would eventually be limited, I found keeping my mind active was of more use in maintaining my purity.

Back at the end of high school, it was at that SU Discipleship Camp that I met a young lady by the name of Adrienne. I had my eyes on someone else at the time so did not really pay too much attention except to note that here was a nice young lady. At that time, we were both single and certainly enjoying life as single people.

Adrienne puts forward a slightly different story, however. She tells me that she noticed me but accepted that my eyes were diverted elsewhere, and I was unavailable. It was ironic that I had been in the hospital less than two weeks before camp due to that mystery numbness in my legs (the onset of my MS—I just did not know it for another three years). So, in fact, Adrienne has known me for the entire duration of my MS journey, from the very first step of my answer to prayer for a rushing wind.

The campers who attended this camp formed a tight group and decided to spend our Schoolies Week at the SU camp of the same name up at the Sunshine Coast. By this stage, the girl I had my eyes set on had moved overseas with her family to prepare for missionary service. Adrienne was once again present to enjoy our time as a group but continued to accept the status quo. Mind you, she accepted the fact but was still able to enjoy life as a single young lady. Looking back, this time could be referred to as 'the wait that continued needlessly.' When would I see reason?

Then when university began, a number of the old Discipleship Camp group studied together on the St Lucia campus of the University of Queensland. We all joined a Christian group known as ES, where we would often reminisce about the fun that we had on those grade-twelve camps.

The opportunity arose during one of our frequent nostalgic moments for me to suggest, "How about we have a five-year reunion of Discipleship

Camp!" Another excuse for a university social event. In the meantime, I had left home, moved around a bit, and eventually moved into a share-house situation, so we met at my rental property for a reunion.

Dating had not been very successful for me since beginning university, and I was currently single as of six months earlier. I remember the two of us spending most of the night talking. No one had a chance to talk to either of us that night because we hardly paused. It was at this reunion that we clicked, but I had been deeply hurt during my breakup, so I was turned off relationships of any sort. I was still emotionally raw and not ready for any romantic relationship. Once more, Adrienne was there, but I was still not ready, so she just had to wait. You may say the real wait began here, but in reality, Adrienne happily continued to live her single life to the fullest as an independent young woman. I was available but not ready. It was just a matter of time until I was convinced and ready (like I have heard it referred to, in relation to waiting for a man to realize and be convinced that he needed to marry that special girl—she would just need to wait it out until the male saw sense)! While Adrienne had to wait, I needed a good clout to the back of the head to wake me up.

A little less than a year later, after several housemates got married or moved on, I was renting the same house on my own and working away at my research thesis for a Bachelor of Dental Studies degree. I was becoming more content not to go out but to stay at home like a hermit, keeping busy with my studies and my church ministries of Sunday School and PA. I even confided in prayer with God one evening that I was happy to remain single. I prayed that if God wanted me to be anything other than single, He would have to do two things (like we can give God conditions!)

1. She would have to make the first move.
2. She would have to catch my attention.

Then one night a few months later, while I was doing some work on my computer, the phone rang. I was about to get that clout! It was Adrienne. She was calling to catch up and see how I was doing. Her uncle in England had MS, and I had come to mind following an Easter message at her church.

We talked and talked. She had rung at about 8:30 p.m., and when I hung up, the clock on the wall had just clicked past midnight. I remember thinking she seemed like a really nice girl when I met her at the end of high school. And we had talked very easily at the Discipleship reunion. I had never thought anything more of it, but after my prayer a few months before, I could not help but think, *Well, she made the first move, and she grabbed my attention.* (We had talked for over three hours.) *Still,* I thought, *I'm not going to rush into anything.* You would think I would finally take the hint! But no!

I would soon be moving into a new house, so I invited Adrienne to come over for a coffee once I had moved in. If her call had come a couple of months later, I would have already moved, and we would have been unlikely to cross paths again. I would be responsible for closing the door and missing the boat permanently.

We were meant to be together, and God prompted her to make that first move. It was almost as if, with a bit of divine help, she became sick of waiting! God was faithful to pick up the slack when I did not get on board with the program. He took over. It seemed like she had to almost invite herself into my life because I was not making any moves. But it was an invitation I would never regret!

Shortly after this, we started dating, but then she went over to the UK for a long planned holiday (originally it had been open-ended, but thankfully it was shortened to a four-month stay). During that time, I came to a point of knowing that Adrienne was indeed the one God had for me. I finally woke up, came to my senses, and joined the program.

In general conversation before she left, I had assured Adrienne that I could never propose to a girl within the first twelve months of dating; we would have a chance to get to know each other in different circumstances as life happens. At the time, Adrienne had agreed with this logic, so when she returned, I waited impatiently for that twelve-month deadline. Ironically, I found that the shoe was now on the other (my) foot, and I was *so* conscious of it! But I just had to wait.

On our twelve-month anniversary, she came over, and I cooked dinner at my place. Then we retired to relax on the couch to talk. During our conversation, I suddenly remembered my promise and realized the significance that this evening held. On recalling this, my impatience became uncontrollable, so I blurted out eagerly, "Adrienne, it's been twelve months, and I said I could never ask you before now, but will you marry me?" It was the most unromantic proposal you could ever imagine. It is amazing what can happen, despite not having patience or the romantic bent to go away and plan something special. Thank goodness she did not stand on tradition for me to arrange an elaborate proposal.

Understandably, she was more than a bit surprised, but I like to say she got me back for all of those years of delay by asking for time to think it over (which was to be expected, considering my request, especially with my positive diagnosis of MS). As hard as it was, that is exactly what I had to do—wait! It was definitely my turn now. I needed patience. But when I think about how many chances and opportunities passed by over that decade, the least I could do was wait while she thought it over. I can truly say that God was indeed good to bring us together despite my distraction and faltering confidence and patience after we first met!

A week later, I was over at her house when she presented me with a stuffed pig (the movie *Babe* had just been released in the cinemas) with a note attached saying "This Babe needs a home." She said, "Yes!" The wait was over, but now, all I could say was, "Are you sure?" (I had convinced myself that she world probably say, 'No' to help minimize the disappointment when the inevitable turn down happened.) She said that she knew what the MS meant, but when she thought about the difficulties with the MS as opposed to living a life without me, she decided that she did not want to live life with a missed opportunity. And that has characterized the devotion and commitment with which she has blessed me ever since.

So, after an impatient ten-month engagement, we got married in September 1999. During our wedding ceremony, my song "Take Hold" was performed. It was a special time because in a way, those words summarized well the importance of taking hold of the opportunity that had been placed in our life paths to join together before God in the act of holy matrimony. It was also an opportunity to once more implore those who were present who did not have a personal relationship with God to take hold of that moment now before it was too late!

Three months later, I finally graduated with a Bachelor of Dental Science degree after nine years, closing one part of my life and beginning a new chapter with Adrienne. God was faithful and good to me. I must have run God's patience to the utter limit before I got on board with His plan. But once I did, I never looked back. She was and still is a perfect gift and my best friend with whom to share my life.

14

Children

Children are a heritage
from the LORD,
offspring a reward from Him.
—Psalm 127:3

Another way that we saw God's goodness was in the gift of children following our marriage. Several years after we began life together, my wife and I developed a deep desire to have children. This would become another brick in my life.

I realize that not all people will have children, either through choice or circumstances, and this brick is missing (according to our mortal perspective). There are times when dreams are broken or do not even get off the ground. Times when the dream of offspring can only be entertained, nothing more. When we may have said, "God, this is not fair! You give us a glimpse (or taste/hunger) of the promised land and then rip it away." And it is all right to say this to God. He understands. These times are an ideal opportunity for God to build a window! An opportunity for God to make you the best person you can be, living your life to the fullest in whatever situation you find yourself, be it married or single, parents or DINKs (double income, no kids), able-bodied or disabled. God gives special grace to anyone when needed so that they may find fulfilment despite circumstances, so long as they leave themselves open for Him to work.

A life without children looked like it may be the case for us. When we began trying for a family, we were restricted to using science through the In Vitro Fertilization (IVF) method, which has at its best a success rate of only 40 percent.

We both have a strong belief that life begins upon conception, and this would influence our decisions during the IVF process. In pursuing a family, we were careful about how many embryos would be created during each cycle to ensure that no excess embryos would be formed so that they would never be discarded, because they were lives regardless of their size. And so, as a matter of conviction, we would naturally implant every life that had been created and let God be God and decide if any were to be successful. On principle and practicality, we would only fertilize that number of eggs (to form embryos) that we would then be willing to have implanted and have added to our family. But we would give them all the chance to live. And by default, this meant that we would never have to face the question of what to do with excess embryos. Because we knew what the answer would be—we could never on principle simply discard them! So potentially, if we were not careful, we could overstretch ourselves beyond our capacity to support a family. We would never let this eventuate.

As a result, that success rate dropped significantly below 40 percent. Our stance made it more difficult to attain success, and each negative result usually ended in us being deposited right back at square one, needing to begin the whole process once more. It also meant that the resources from that attempt would be lost—resources that were limited to begin with. We only had a certain number of attempts available to us. But we felt strongly and were willing to say to God, "If You want us to have a family, we know that You will provide. If not, we will accept Your will." This would have its full impact years later (see next chapter, "Satisfied," chapter 15).

For now, after several false starts, our first son, Nathan, was conceived relatively quickly (as we would later discover, compared to our long-term journey) after only three failed assisted cycles and on the second full IVF cycle. Things had been much easier than the stereotypical process of IVF, and this would increase the despair we would feel later. But for now, we were thankful! God had blessed us with our first child.

There are numerous challenges in pursuing an IVF method of conception, but there were also a few advantages. Following a confirmed successful implantation, we had the opportunity to view an ultrasound of our son at a very early stage when he was only four weeks old (six weeks gestational). We did not have to wait until the usual twenty-week scan. Following a blood test, we presented for a primary ultrasound.

As we looked at the screen, the disappointments of failed attempts faded into obscurity to be replaced by the image of a gray jellybean on a black screen with a small pulsating white dot (the heart) near one end. It was a special time. This was one of the critical signs of life medically, the presence of a heartbeat. Even at this early stage, here was strong proof of life! Confirmation of our conviction! We had a child, a real, living child! Wow!

This fact would have further ramifications as far as treatment for my neurological disease as well, since embryonic stem cell therapies (ESCT) rely on destructive harvesting of cells from early-stage embryos. Early stage but a life nonetheless as shown by the presence of a heartbeat. And so this was and still is out of the question for us. But more about that later (see "Healing," chapter 19).

Adrienne's pregnancy went well with no illness or complications. I decided to work at strengthening myself in preparation for children in an attempt to ease the burden for Adrienne. So I set about intensive physiotherapy, because that was all I could do (if only you could snap your fingers). Despite my best attempt, I saw no dramatic improvement so felt significantly underprepared as the day approached. How would I be able to support and assist Adrienne? What could I offer? However, God had shown Himself faithful in giving us a child. I knew He would be faithful to help me support her when she needed it.

Despite feeling underprepared and inadequate, the birth continued to approach. No one is ever fully ready for their first child though, are they? All I could do was dive in as best I could. More of a belly flop really! I coped amazingly well following the birth. I received strength and endurance right when I needed. This allowed me, despite my feelings, to support Adrienne as best I could as she went through the usual roller coaster in learning to care for a first child. She had a caesarian delivery, and we then followed a piece of advice we had been given that "deep down, you feel and know what you should do", and so we became a family of three. Accepting advice when offered but filtering everything with common sense and that deep feeling—a mother's intuition.

When Nathan reached about eighteen months of age, we began trying for a second child. Time had dulled the memories of surgical delivery, and Nathan had come along relatively easily in our recollections such that we had been lulled into a false sense that this IVF stuff was not so bad, for us anyway. As a result, we came down with a hard landing when it took nearly four years for Matthew to come along.

At first, it seemed that it would be easy. There was a successful implantation, and all seemed to be going well. So well in fact that one Friday night in August 2006, I committed with Adrienne's blessing to help out at a children's program at our church. Adrienne stayed home to rest.

At heart, I am an extrovert, so I came home with a buzz after being out at a high-energy children's night. When I walked through the door, I hit the ground hard. Instead of a joyful greeting with a smile, she greeted me with tear-streaked cheeks. While I was out, she had miscarried. I was tormented with the thought of, *If only I had been there!* I felt useless as we cried for the next few hours, embraced, and mourned. There was nothing I could have done, but it just kept running through my mind on continual play.

Eventually, we went to bed. We were emotionally and physically exhausted. There was nothing more that could be achieved by sitting up. So we retired for a night of restless sleep. Lying in bed after more tears and a final good night, the light went out, and I lay in the dark numb and silent. Unable to put into words what I was feeling, I had the same question repeating itself in my head, "What if I had not gone?" Adrienne, feeling the palpable silence, asked me what I was thinking because there was no way I could have dropped off to sleep so quickly, considering what had just happened.

At first, I could not even catch my breath. What could I say? It felt like we had been dropped from the top of the skyscraper, back to square one all over again. The added kick in the stomach came with having been blessed with a real live child and positive pregnancy only to endure the cruelty of having it taken away. After a while, I was able to get control of my breathing and choke out in a whisper, "All I can say is - God is still good!"

If only I had been there, I could not have done something, anything to stop it. But the only thing I could now do was to repeat a single fact that I knew for certain over and over again in my mind. Even in our pain, the only words I was able to verbalize was something that I knew for a fact. God is still good! It was something I had to say. Not just for Adrienne but for myself as well. It was the only thing I could form into something like a prayer. To say, "God, I know you are still good!" In the years to come, there would be times when words could not be found to express our feelings or desires. But it is good to know that the Spirit "intercedes for us with groanings that cannot be uttered" (Rom 8:26).

The following week while driving to my weekly physiotherapy appointment, the song "Praise You in the Storm"[21] by Casting Crowns from their 2005 album *Lifesong* came over the radio waves. It was the first time I had heard this song, and as the first verse and chorus ended, the words began to sink in, and I had to pull over to the side of the road, as I could not see clearly to drive because of the tears that flooded out. It had been three days since Adrienne had miscarried, and I thought that, as in the song, surely God would have embraced us and wiped away our tears. I knew that He could reach down to step in if there was something He wanted to teach us. However, I found that days later, the pain continued without ceasing. In the middle of the turmoil, I listened to the words of the song, which reminded me of my longing to hear His whisper, "I'm with you." But for now, it seemed that there was only silence!

As I sat there in the car, I felt His mercy wash over me. And as I let the words of that song sink in, I found that they prompted a heartfelt response. I let go of the steering wheel to turn my hands heavenward and praise the God who had first given and then taken away. It sounded like a total contradiction to praise Him for doing so. But God is God, He is who He is, His ways are not our ways, and I was reminded that no matter what I was going through, He knew it all. This situation may not be taken away, but He was with us catching every tear and holding each one. I could trust Him, and despite my heartache, I could praise Him. It went on poetically to encourage me as in Psalm 121:1–2, that when "I lift up my eyes to the hills… my help comes from the Lord, who made heaven and earth" (NRSV).

I still had that guilt floating around in my mind: *I should have been there*. I wanted to be strong for Adrienne so made a conscious effort to not unload my own pain and emotions. It was in this experience that I felt God's hand on my shoulder as He said to me, "It's okay. I know!" Indeed, it was time to raise my hands in praise, because He is sovereign, He is faithful, and He cares! Eventually, after taking a deep breath, I pulled back out into the traffic with strength to move forward, support Adrienne, and keep trying.

15

Satisfied

Be content with what God gives.

During the period when we were trying for a second child, I cannot take credit for supporting Adrienne. There would inevitably be a significant song of praise/comfort, comments in sermons, passages of scripture, excerpts from books, or commentary from the radio to encourage us as we walked this journey to remind us that we were not walking the road alone. Together with scripture, these songs, insights, and glimmers of light acted as pillars of strength and encouragement upon which we learned to cry out affirmations during times of pain and disappointment. And this would naturally help us to put our feelings into words. There was no more trying to shelter the other one from your pain. God can take all the credit. He was faithful! And in the end, He did grant to us the desires of our hearts.

Fast forward, and by 2007, we had tried numerous times to fall pregnant once more, but nothing had been successful. We had tried repeatedly, with different methods, techniques, variations, and combinations thereof but all to no avail. We had a limited budget, resources, and time, so each failure that meant being sent back to square one impacted us like a piledriver and intensified the question in our minds of, *What if they are all unsuccessful?* Each time, we would enter a fresh cycle with renewed hope, only to have it crushed in some way.

For example, on one occasion, two embryos were implanted in an earlier fresh cycle that had been unsuccessful. We were starting to expect the worst and so had two additional eggs frozen for a future attempt if needed. And when that fresh cycle was unsuccessful, we used those two frozen eggs in another attempt. The eggs had been thawed and fertilized successfully the day before, but when we went in for implantation, we were told that after the twenty-four-hour mark when we had received the telephone call with an update and were advised to come in, neither embryo had continued to grow. This was devastating news for us. Yet again it had been unsuccessful, and we were another step closer to the end of our dream. We did not want it to be true, but it was fact. We should be thankful for one child, shouldn't we? It was hard to be thankful at that moment. It was hard to praise in the midst of that storm!

After being given time to grieve alone in a private back room, we still had those two embryos implanted, as there was a minuscule chance that they may "wake up". It was like implanting something doomed to failure, but we felt that while there was any chance at all, we could not just walk away and let these tiny lives go. We still praised God that there were two embryos full stop, but we had few expectations and were not surprised at a negative pregnancy test a few days later.

Then shortly after this, a chorus was sung in church, originally sung by Matt Redman, that I had heard years previously, and now considering what had just occurred, the words took on a whole new significance. This song was titled "Blessed Be Your Name"[22] from his album *Where Angels Fear to Tread*. Based on Job's response to all of the bad news that he received, "the Lord gave and the Lord has taken away; may the name of the Lord be praised" (Job 1:21). He begins by pointing out that we bless His name when all is good, plentiful, and abundant. We had been blessed with one child (Nathan) already, but we could still praise and bless His name when we walked through the desert and wilderness. This felt like it was the case now, with every attempt ending in failure. We had received blessings during which naturally we had praised God. Now, when darkness came, we still needed to remember to always praise Him. His name is to be blessed!

Then the words of Job are repeated to God Himself and the reassurance that it is our choice to praise His name—a choice that we will make.

As the song played, all I could do was sit and read the words as I sang in my heart. Anything more, and I would not have been able to hold it together. I would have broken down and wept. Such was the significance of these words—to be reminded that we could still say with Job, "The Lord gave and the Lord has taken away; may the name of the Lord be praised" (Job 1:21). Both when we were on the highs and when the darkness seemed to close in, this was all we could do. And as we listened to the melodic words, all we could do was reach out and grasp one another's hands tightly and cling to God, knowing that He was sovereign.

For the next two years, we continued attempting to fall pregnant without success and without hearing any distinct messages. Each time, we stepped closer to that final moment when we would exhaust all of our resources and finances. Late in 2008, we did in fact reach the end, as we began what would be our final fresh cycle. This meant that we were about to draw a line under the idea of having children (plural) if the results continued to be negative throughout these last few attempts.

The week before we were due to go for the blood test in that final fresh cycle, I came across a song by Steven Curtis Chapman called "God Is God"[23] from his 2001 album, *Declaration*. It talks of how pain would fall like a curtain on a stage, obscuring long-known certainties. I was sure that it was meant to give me strength before that time when we would approach the end of our dream. We would have to admit something that as humans we find hard to do because His ways are not our ways. The chorus states the truth that God is God, and as humans, we are not. He then goes on to use the illustration of God painting a picture (our lives), yet we never see the whole picture.

As mortals, we see only one part of it because we're not God. So, despite the outcome now, we could not presuppose the eventual destination while still on that road. Only He sees the whole picture as He paints it and so understands it all. I was sure that this song was preparing me for a negative result once more by reminding me of God's sovereignty.

He closes the song in praise of His wisdom and knowledge before repeating the concluding lines of the doxology of Romans 11:36, saying, "For from Him and through Him and for Him are all things. To Him be the glory forever!" In previous years, we found that there had always been something (a song, a message, a verse, a book … something) just before or after some critical turn in the road. And yet again, it seemed like we were being prepared for that daunting outcome.

Without verbalizing our fears, we began to affirm to each other that even if we never had more children, this would be okay if it was God's will. Whatever the outcome now, we would take as God's sovereign will, and we knew that His plan and will are always perfect and good. Even if we did not understand it, all we could do was hold His hand. And this, in fact, is what did eventuate. Sure enough, after this, we continued to receive negative results as we used those last few frozen eggs (once more, we had frozen as many unfertilized eggs/embryos as we dared), bringing us ever closer to the eventual curtain drop.

Ultimately, in March 2009 following failure after failure, we had a single embryo left frozen from the previous fresh cycle, and we felt ready to say that if this was not successful, then we would accept that it was not God's plan for us to have more than one child. We would draw a line under the dream and allow the door to be closed and the curtain dropped with a sense of peace. And that was okay; we were so thankful for our beautiful son, Nathan, and we had come to the point where we were happy in whatever direction we were led.

When we began this final attempt, I knew God had encouraged and spoken to us through all the previous cycles in some way, and so I began an intensive search to look for what He would use this time, hoping to get a sneak peek at what the answer would be. I listened attentively to everything I heard and paid special attention to everything I read. But there were no songs, no verses, and no books that caught my eye as previously. There was only silence. Nothing! It seemed like God's mouth was sealed. We had the embryo implanted, but even searching everywhere, all we heard was deafening silence. I just had that assurance that I had seen affirmed in everything over the previous six months: God is sovereign! But would that be enough for us now?

I shared this to encourage Adrienne, saying, "If this is His will, it will happen in spite of anything (e.g. weight, diet, nutrition, or anything else). If it is *not* His will, there is nothing we can do to make it happen!" She added the extra affirmation, "And He will never give more than we can handle."

And this was our mantra right through that final attempt. Despite there being no songs, no messages, no thoughts, and no voices, there was one simple statement that we held on to: God is sovereign! And I thought that was it! I could not get past the belief that God was preparing us for yet another inevitable negative result once more. (I did not share that thought with Adrienne, for fear of crushing her hopes and dreams. I saw my role as an encourager, not a destroyer).

That year I bought a movie for Adrienne's birthday. She had wanted the movie *Fireproof* for her birthday ever since going to a Casting Crowns concert, so when I got it, I also got *Facing the Giants* by the same production company for Nathan to give her as a present. I later thought better of it and got something more suitable for him to give her, but she still received it as part of my present to her. You might ask, *Why on earth would I give my wife a DVD about American Gridiron for her birthday?-It sounds like a typical husband gift of a bowling ball from a tenpin bowling enthusiast to his wife so that he could get a new bowling ball!* There had been no rhyme or reason in my decision to choose that particular DVD. But when we finally got around to watching it, we realized that it had been God's leading. So, in a way, you could blame Him!

The storyline, about a couple trying to fall pregnant via the IVF path as we were and the way they eventually said to God, "Whatever comes, I will still praise you!" encouraged us immensely. In our own way, we came to this same point in our IVF journey. Just as Jesus had prayed in the Garden of Gethsemane, 'Not my will, but Yours' (Luk 22:42b), though our desire was to have more than one child, we wanted whatever was God's will for us. And we would praise Him no matter what. Our gynecologist had been unsatisfied with the hormone levels, so we delayed for yet another month. But then, after implantation, came the moment of truth when we would receive the ominous blood test and results. We had been reminded that we needed to praise Him regardless of the outcome. And positive or negative, we were already satisfied!

16

The Silence of God

Sometimes God may remain silent until we are ready to listen.

After what seemed like months of silence, when we had that final blood test, we saw God move! The morning we were due to find out the results for our last-ditch IVF attempt, we rose early and went in to town for the pregnancy test. On our way home, we went out for breakfast, then stopped in at a local Christian bookstore to get a CD for Nathan. I stayed in the car while Adrienne took Nathan into the store. Getting restless, I checked my phone and found there had been two missed calls. When they returned to the car, I shared this news with Adrienne, and we immediately raced home and tried to return the call, only to find that the pathology rooms had closed.

We rang the doctors' rooms, hoping that they may be able to put us out of our misery, whatever the news, good or bad. This is when we heard the words, "Congratulations! The test shows a strong positive!" Those words were so overpowering. Adrienne was definitely pregnant! It had been our very last chance with our very last embryo. If this had not been successful, the IVF process would get a lot more complicated from then on, so it would not be possible for us to continue, which would mean a closed door, a dropped curtain. However it was put, it would be the end of our IVF journey.

After nearly four years of trying, God had granted our hearts' desire. I was in tears, weeping for joy. All I could get out was, "I'm overwhelmed!" I just repeated it again and again while I rocked backward and forward, tears rolling freely down my face. I wept in praise, joy, and awe for what must have been twenty minutes. Nathan even asked Adrienne, "Is Daddy all right? Why is he crying? Don't cry Daddy. It's all right." I had to laugh and assure him that I was crying because I was happy, not because I was sad.

During our IVF journey, it seemed like there were times when God did not come through with an answer when I prayed. It was not simply that we would not get enough of the details fast enough. No, there would be no discernible answer at all. They were times when I would cry out pleading for a positive outcome, and my prayers instead would become a plea for an answer of any kind. "Just answer one way or the other—*please!*" A negative answer was at least an answer. But on some attempts, we did not have any indication of what the outcome would be until we received those negative answers.

My prayers felt like they were bouncing off the ceiling. There had been other times in my life when I had cried out in desperation, "I need You to come through now; otherwise, I don't think I'll make it." And I had found that God was always there regardless of what I felt. You would think I would learn, but we humans are sometimes so slow to learn. Thank goodness God is patient!

We all have such moments in our lives. Moments when we cry out, "How much more? They are wanting me to do X, but there is no way that I have it within me to do it. I do not know what I should do." We can take an earnest request to God, and He may say, "Yes! Finally, he has exhausted all of his resources. Now I can act!" And He then speaks to us, or He does act. But before this, it seems like there is silence. He is simply waiting until we see and admit that without Him, we will not make it.

Moments when we may take one step forward, only to be knocked two steps back. When we may start to look to Him. Just as the disciples on the rough sea did not recognize that it was Jesus walking out on the water because they were not looking for Him until the very end. Their attention was turned to the wind and the waves. It was not until they were at their end that they were ready for Him to act. Likewise, sometimes we never know Him as deeply until the only resource remaining for us is Him. Then we rely on nothing else.

For some, this may come naturally through growing in their Christian walk. There are others who may find this deepening relationship in the midst of the storms of life. For some, like myself, the lessons are not learned without a bit of what I have called dynamite. God becomes the ultimate architect if rebuilds are needed.

In both growing maturity and storms, God is reliable and faithful as the source of strength. I think I needed both that bit of dynamite as well as the inevitable storms of life in order for growth to occur. When I left home, slowly but surely, I exhausted all of my resources until the only place I could turn was to God, after which He could speak and lead without interruption. Now, our experience in the IVF journey had striking echoes. It seemed that God had been silent, we reached the end of our resources, and only then did we see Him move. You would think I could say, "I've been there, done that, and got the T-shirt." But in the midst of a storm, I did not take time to think of previous experiences.

If we talk about silence as being like a coin, one side may be where the answers are uncertain and we need to stay even closer to Him while we wait for some kind of answer. And on the other side of it, there are times when you may be certain of what God wants or where He is leading (times that do not necessarily need dynamite to clear out an overgrown and messy plot of land), but it feels like all you are doing is pushing against a solid brick wall of silence. Nothing seems to give way, and any prayer that you send up seems to just bounce back off the ceiling. Where is that dynamite to work in your favor when you need it? So, what do you do when you know from earlier God-things that the answer is positive? Keep pushing on! Just as I did with study. We all go through times of solid brick walls and rebounding ceilings.

During different times along our IVF journey, we experienced both sides of the same coin—times when God wanted us to rely more fully on Him while we waited for some kind of guidance. Or times when we were certain that we should continue, but we simply had to wait for an answer, be it positive or not. As we would discover, a delay did not mean that God had deserted us, was not listening, or that the answer was, 'No'.

Silence can mean various things at various times. Silence may mean that the time is not right (as in Jesus's delay going to Lazarus when he was sick), or He wants to teach us something (like Peter walking to Jesus on the waves), or He wants to help us grow further (just like the disciples on the stormy sea). One thing is certain though. He will answer the humble and sincere plea—just maybe not according to our timetable, but He is always there. The one thing in common is the matter of waiting. Waiting to see whether the answer is positive or negative, but even more, waiting to see what answer will be given for what reason. It was and is a matter of waiting.

Despite not hearing an answer to a question/prayer, we can still know without a doubt that He is there. He is consistent and does not change. He "is the same yesterday, today and forever" (Heb 13:8). So, if He has revealed His plans and directions to us, and we have heard this correctly, we can be sure that He will not change those directions. As a result, we can push on with certainty and confidence. Yes, this had been the case with my study years before and yet again with the IVF. Once more, there was certainty during uncertainty. We could at least persist in our requests despite apparent silence, knowing that we would be following a biblical principle, just as the widow persisted in seeking justice (Luk 18:1–8).

The day after we heard from God and saw Him move was Easter Sunday, and I was still emotional and choking up as I gave thanks for breakfast (Adrienne had to finish for me). The sermon at church was about how we may face obstacles in our lives, but Jesus has already won the victory for us. As the persistent widow, we can succeed with Him. Coincidentally, over the preceding weeks, I had been doing extraordinarily well in my physiotherapy sessions as once more I began to prepare for a hopeful pregnancy following a prayer for healing. (See "Healing", chapter 19.) After we got the news of success, we heard this message. It was a most poignant way to cap off some wonderful news!

The words of Isaiah 55 come to mind again, that our ways are not God's ways. Sometimes, what seems like God's delays do not mean God's denial. We cannot always understand His ways. All we can do, all we are asked to do, is keep asking and petitioning God and then wait for His timing. But then when the answer is given, all we should do is accept it and bless Him. He is sovereign, and His ways are best.

There was another type of silence that I was yet to experience. And along with this came the need for patience as I waited. With MS, there are always things you wish you could do but are unable to. I have learned to be satisfied (at least I've tried to be) with the fact that I can hear about events once they are finished and people return home, as far as family goes. You have to be satisfied with doing what you can as for the Lord. There would be times in years to come (as far as ministry went) when I was able to do or give less (just like the widow offering two small coins).

There was soon to be another reminder to me of how little I was able to give and my need to depend on God. Remember, I like to at least hear about events once they have finished, if I cannot attend. Sometimes, as much as this is still heart-wrenching, I have had to be satisfied with the fact that I can only do what I can. Not more! When it came to Matthew's birth, once more, we chose to have an elective caesarean, just as we had with Nathan.

Due to my decreased capacity and my limited ability to help care for Adrienne following a major operation, we decided that I should spend two weeks in respite care. I found this a most difficult period of separation when it would be at least thirty-six hours before I could even present myself in person for any kind of debrief or opportunity to meet my new son or daughter. I remember waking up one morning and waiting for someone to come and get me up to shower me. I looked at the clock and thought, *Adrienne will be in presurgery right now, and our child may even be delivered already.* Was it a boy? Was it a girl?

Yet again, silence can be insufferable when you are in the middle of it. I understood how grandparents must feel as they wait for word of a birth. But this was my own child! The news was wonderful. It was a boy! And once I heard that everything went well and both Adrienne and Matthew were safe and healthy, I just wanted to see them as soon as possible. It could not happen immediately, but it did happen in time! This was just one example where we needed to do what was needed. It was not always easy. Invariably, it would be a reminder to me that I was no longer able to do what I wanted, how I wanted, or when I wanted. I needed and still need to wait.

Among many things, I have learned patience—certainly not perfectly, but I am getting there. Slowly! It was also at this point when I found that my love of Christian music from a very early age played a great role in uplifting me. I did not gain my direct theology by listening to these songs, but they did remind me of the truths that I relied on while I waited, and this helped me put everything in perspective. I remember a saying by Joni Eareckson Tada that she often prays while she is being dressed and prepared for another day in her wheelchair as a quadriplegic, "O God, please, may I borrow your smile?"[24] I am reminded that "with God all things are possible" (Matt 19:26). I can face the day ahead in His strength.

This may have been our journey to have children as a couple, but for me, it was a journey to understand more completely God's sovereignty and to grow closer to God. For others, the circumstances may be different, but the lessons are the same. It is not until we have nothing that both we and God can begin. And then you can see God move, though not necessarily in line with what your expectations are. He is God; we are not. For us, it seemed that it was not until we were wholly satisfied with a potential and likely negative result that we saw God work on that very last chance. Yes, God was faithful!

My journey is not yet complete and will not be until I reach heaven. I may not see the full picture, but that is okay with me. I know, God is faithful and can be trusted despite "silence", so He can be blessed and praised! My place for now is to listen and be prepared to move when He says, "Move", and not to be afraid to keep knock, knock, knocking!

I have truly found that God is not a God who is silent. We may not always hear His voice or feel the hands of His love. When we do not hear His voice, we may not be listening, or there may be too much background noise in life around us. At other times, it may seem that God is silent because we have no definite answer about something we have been praying fervently about. It has been said that there are three answers that God can give to our prayer requests: 'Yes', 'No', and 'Wait'. Sincere prayer will always receive one of these three answers. And I have learned that God's silence is not necessarily a denial. If all you hear is silence, wait! But be persistent in your requests. There will be an answer in God's time.

17

The Voice of God

When God talks,
our job is to listen and obey!

There are many ways in which God speaks to us: dreams and visions, voices (although not always audibly), circumstances, those around us, His Word (preaching or reading), to name just a few. A number of years before my marriage to Adrienne and our pursuit of parenthood, one evening in a small two-room granny flat I heard God's response to a cry from my heart when He told me, "You Are Mine." It was the first time of only a handful that I have heard what I refer to as the voice of God. While not an audible voice, it was a deep sense and absolute conviction of knowing God's heart and will. At these times, although it may not have been audible, it was as if I did hear an audible voice; my mind was so certain of the words. At other times, I would experience the protective wing of God as He cradled me close after concerted and earnest prayer during lonely, agonizing moments. Each time I have experienced these moments, they have been pivotal in knowing God's will and following His direction for my life.

I may have first heard the voice of God in a small granny flat, but this has not been the only way that God has communicated with me. I have heard it suggested that if you pray earnestly as you go to sleep, your mind can switch off while your subconscious continues to pray and petition God. And He can give the answer either shortly after you wake up or even by waking you from slumber with the answer. Or another way to receive an answer is by giving it to you in a dream/vision. Once my life was once again on an even keel, in addition to hearing God's assurance, I heard His direction in the still of the night.

A while after getting married, a visiting speaker came to our church. He spoke on letting God use us in spite of who we are. I approached him at the conclusion of the service to share the struggle that I was going through at the time, feeling useless for God since I felt I could do less and less because I was more restricted in what I could do physically. We prayed, and he advised me to look for opportunities that God put in my path and to serve everywhere I could.

I threw myself into service at church as much as I could. At that time, I had been serving as the head of our Sunday School. Child safety was becoming an important issue in all forms of children's work, so I became heavily involved in drafting and writing initial policy documents for our church. In days to come, I would find out what the advice concerning "looking for opportunities" really meant.

A few months later, as I was concentrating on a job (after graduating, I began working as an office administrator for Adrienne when she started an accountancy business, in preparation for the day when I would need twenty-four-hour care at home), and I received a phone call from our senior pastor. I was feeling pressured to get my work done but felt that I should take the call and not put him off. It was a good thing that I took the call, as God was about to place an opportunity in my path.

Our pastor asked if I would be willing to serve on a committee that would collate previous reports on our church governance systems that had been commissioned at various times over the previous twenty years. Our job would be to look at the recommendations, assess what was still relevant, make current proposals, and guide/direct the restructuring of those systems. I was humbled that he felt I had something to offer, and then to be asked left me without words. I was feeling like I had little to offer except teaching children (a warped perception of how important this ministry is and how significant it can be, a prejudiced view that never held water). I told him that I would pray about it even though privately, with the way I had been feeling lately, I thought that I had little or nothing to offer and would simply be wasting space.

That night, my head could not hit the pillow fast enough. It had been a busy and demanding day. I wanted to get to sleep, but that phone call was playing on my mind. I had promised that I would pray over the issue. There was no better time than now, so after the lights went off and everything went quiet, I took the opportunity to pray in the stillness about whether this was something that I could do and whether God wanted me to do it. The last thing I remember was my prayer. I must have continued praying as I dropped off to sleep. Later that night, I woke up, and I felt God telling me that I should accept this position. What followed was a Moses-like argument with God. Guess who won?

> *"But I have MS. I am not physically able."*
> **"I will give you the strength that you require."**

> *"But I can't fulfil this role with any quality."*
> **"You have the intelligence given by Me. You have written a full thesis and other policy documents."**

> *"But I really can't do this."*
> **"What I have directed, you *CAN* do with *Me*."**

After all of my weak excuses, He shut down my arguments with one simple statement. I backed off and immediately stopped arguing and accepted His direction. I went back to sleep with a peace that God was directing me to take part in this committee. The next day, I got up, rang the pastor, and shared the story about my futile debate the night before. I told him to give my answer to the Pastoral Team, and then he shared with me that all the people consulted had been enthusiastically supportive of his asking me. Even if I did not have it, they had confidence in me. As it turned out, I was able to play a significant role in the drafting, producing, and writing of those new policy documents for the church, and I played a role in that committee that I never could have imagined.

It was an example of keeping watch for opportunities and then being willing to jump, just as I had been told all those months before. It was a matter of persistently offering myself for service while remaining open to any opportunities that may present themselves. In this case, where I had needed to wait even though there were no feelings of usefulness, it came down to a matter of faith, knowing that at the right time, God would use me as and how He so wished.

A little over a year after these changes were adopted by the church and implemented, I was again phoned as I was about to leave one morning for a men's Bible study that I had joined. It was our senior pastor once more. He explained that when nominations had been called and considered for the church council, it was felt that I should be approached. I distinctly remember my response. "My first thought is that I am honored that someone thinks I am suitable for the position. The second—I don't think

I can fulfill that role. But the third is that over the last two to three years, I have learned not to close the door on anything straight away if it is what God wants. So, if I can have some time to pray about it."

Well, I left for the Bible study and prayed the whole way there, saying, "Lord, I feel inadequate for this, but if You want me to do it, please show me and assure me." We were doing a study on 'Jesus the Healer', and there was the story of a man named Jordan Rubin who at the age of nineteen dropped to a weight of one hundred pounds with nineteen diagnosed diseases. After the preliminary introduction, the picture on the television dropped out. And by the time we got it going again, a picture was being shown, scanning down his body to his feet. I remember thinking, *Boy that looks like me—my body and legs!*

While he shared, he talked about being willing to allow God to work in your life and how he had learned to thank God for those good moments when he was feeling better, the small things he could hold onto. And over time, he found that these moments became longer and longer as God gave him physical strength and healing. He was thankful for what he had, but he still needed faith to step out beyond his current status quo with thanks.

I felt a compelling urge to thank God for my sound mind and intelligence. My body may not work as it should, but my involvement initially in drafting Child Safety protocols and then on that Review Steering Committee (as it became known) had proven to me that I still had a lot to contribute. I just needed to allow God to work through me and be willing to step out of my own status quo. And I needed to be thankful and praise Him when He opened doors for me! Praise Him in all and for all things, whatever may come.

An amazing thing happened a few days later. I contacted our senior pastor to advise him of my positive answer. I then got a hold of the video again so that I could make some notes to remember what had been said. You know how it is said that we all have a twin somewhere in the world? Well, I saw a piece of compelling video footage in support of this. I think I found my twin! I literally was unable to stand up out of my chair for several minutes. I was shaking too much. It was another compelling confirmation that this was a message for me to accept that invitation.

Once I joined the council, I found that indeed I could play a new role as God willed in the strength that He provided. I ended up serving my full four-year term. Now, we had recommended in our new church structure that a sabbatical year should be taken following a term of service. However, there had been a lot of changes within the church in the preceding three and a half years. A new senior pastor had just begun, and there had been nearly a complete turnover of council members, leaving me as the most experienced member.

As the end of my full term approached, I had a growing feeling as I prayed about my future ministry involvement that my role on Council was not yet over. This feeling grew stronger as I continued to pray on it, so I shared it with my wife, who joined me in prayer. With concerted prayer, God revealed the answer to each of us individually, so that when we came to share our feelings together, we found we had a joint confirmation. It even went so far as knowing that God was calling me to extend my term by only two years (no longer). I had no idea why God was saying this to me, but I knew that when He directed something, I was a fool not to listen and obey.

I could not shake this feeling, so I shared at the next Church Council meeting that I would be willing to extend my term by two years if it was felt that this was of God. It was, but the why we still did not know, and the church body agreed, so I stayed on.

Shortly after my term was extended, our church chairman opened a Church Council meeting one evening by sharing with us that he would have to step down as church chairman since he would have to leave the church, having been called elsewhere. As he was talking, I actually felt a tap on my shoulder. I turned to look behind me, only to find there was no one there, but I heard three simple words: "This Is Why!"

Three words, reminiscent of "You Are Mine". I knew it was God giving me the explanation for being called to remain on Council. The next day, I contacted our new senior pastor and offered to stand as interim church chairman if this was acceptable to both the Church Council and church membership. I was humbled when once more there was overwhelming support.

As much as the times that I have described were special, there was no audible voice as such. But I still had unqualified confirmation that left me without any doubt as to what God was saying. As time went by, I had learned to more readily hear, respond to, and obey the voice of God without fighting or arguing. It became a case of "God said it, so I will do it!" When the completion of the extra term approached, the question became, What was God saying now? What did He have in store for me next?

18

The Hands of God

You have not lived today
until you have done something
for someone who can never repay you.

—John Bunyan

Yes, there had been times when I heard what I felt was the voice of God, but there were other times over the years when rather than hearing a voice (audible or otherwise), I would also feel His gentle guiding hand through people, scripture, or circumstances. God's divine power and sovereignty has servants everywhere. It has not always been a case of flashing neon signs that say, "This is the way!"

While my experience had been with unqualified direction as far as my church service went, I know that it is not always so clear for everyone. When God's directions are not so definite, we must be alert to understand when circumstances are actually a form of guidance, direction, or lesson from God.

I have found that being in step with God makes all the difference in knowing His will and direction, even if we do not recognize His direction and guidance. If we walk in union with Him, pay attention, and stay aware, we can receive His encouragement, confirmation, and guidance. We can hear that still small voice.

It may be in hearing that still small voice, or it may be in ways that we see what I call the hands of God (physical demonstrations of the voice of God; we hear one in the heart of our being, and the other we see in the physical world around us). This chapter talks about some of the ways which I have seen the hand of God in my life.

The first example of how I have felt God's hand in my life is through scripture. There have been many times in different circumstances in which

God has spoken to me through His Word. Another thing I am grateful for from my Christian heritage and upbringing is a love for His Word. One incident that stands out to me occurred in 2009 when someone visited me to pray and see how I was doing. It had been nineteen years since the onset of the MS. And as part of that time together, he opened up his Bible to read the passage of Jesus healing the lame man at the pool of Bethesda in John 5:1–15.

I was in the habit of listening with my eyes closed when scripture was read so that nothing distracted me. He got to verse 5, where it states that the man had been lame for thirty-eight years. My eyes shot open as the words sank in. I said jovially, "Wow, I'm halfway there! I've only got nineteen years to go!" If only God was that predictable! But His ways are not our ways.

Another way in which I have seen God lead is when things that have been read and heard can be brought back to memory. As I was considering what my future service within the local church would look like following my time on the Church Council, I remembered hearing that sometimes we may come away from a church service thinking, *That was kind of average. I didn't get much out of it.*

We need to realize that it is not all about us. Sometimes we are at church to edify, encourage, and spur others on. Now, as I finished my upfront role on Church Council, this fact was both an encouragement and direction to me that God could and would still use me behind the scenes so long as I made myself available for Him to use as He wanted.

It was during my experiences with beach missions all those years ago where I was introduced to the concept of intercessory prayer. But it was here that I began to fully appreciate the importance, significance, and reality of it. I have come to learn that although my hands, arms, legs, and voice may not work properly, the mind can still pray for others, as Corrie ten Boom did in her final years (reputedly you would see her eyes move around the room, focusing on prayer points printed on pages stuck up around her room).

And as such, I can still be an encouragement and prayer supporter to fellow travelers while they are on their journey, as Joni Eareckson Tada inspires those going through difficult times. I felt that this was where I was being directed in the future. God could still use me if I made myself available to be used within the scope of my abilities, despite my disabilities. To run the race well. And once more I found a book that was recommended to me by a friend (the biography, *Rees Howells—Intercessor*)[25] was of great significance to me. I felt the hands of God giving me that gentle prod.

I was not always sensitive to those gentle prods though. Over the years, there were numerous times when I needed repeated instructions and reminders from God. Sometimes a prod, sometimes a clout! He would be gracious as I would see His hand on me. Years before my service in church leadership in February 1995, I was at the church I attended prior to my marriage, setting up the PA system for the Sunday-evening service.

It was during those years when I was pursuing a research degree that I continued living my life as if nothing was wrong. The church had a central set of steps leading off the stage. I had been up on stage plugging mics in before heading back to the sound desk. About three or four steps from the bottom, I tripped and went sprawling on the floor at the front of the church.

One thing that my years of playing soccer had taught me was how to fall safely. I immediately went into a tumble roll and ended up flat on my back. I quickly looked around to make sure that there had been no one around to see me make a fool of myself. It was still about two hours before the service. So, as I picked myself up off the floor in the middle of that empty church, I laughed it off, but it certainly gave me a reality check.

One of the doctors, when I was diagnosed, had said simply, "Keep doing as much as you can for as long as you can because if you don't use it, you will lose it." And since I had no noticeable symptoms at the time, I pretty much lived normally, but without the acceptance that I was actually affected.

It was a lesson that needed to be repeated over the years   to do what you can but not more. Otherwise, I would see consequences that I had not planned and could not control. I could not push myself as if nothing was wrong. It was a quick lesson that certainly woke me up and taught me to take notice of the circumstances. I had to learn to do as much as I could but not overdo it. It was a lesson I have never forgotten, although applying it is different from knowing it. I was a slow learner.

At Easter later that year, lessons were learned and repeated. If I had not been alert, I would have missed God's hand of encouragement and direction. My life had been turbulent in the preceding days, but God was about to reveal Himself to me and remind me that although it did not seem like it, He was there every step of the way. And yes, I again needed to slow down and do what I could do, not more.

This was during the period when I had withdrawn from dentistry and was doing research. However, rather than finding it a time to be refreshed and recover from my first-ever relapse, I was actually finding the study/ research more and more taxing. My study/church/life balance was not there. I had been burning the candle at both ends. I had not applied the lesson that I had learned a few months earlier when lying flat on my back at the foot of those steps, to live within my limits. And so my energy reserves instead of being refreshed were being continually depleted.

I eventually recognized this and decided to get things back in balance. Deciding not to go to the usual Good Friday service at church, I spent the weekend praying, reading, studying, fasting, and listening to Christian music to help me refocus on God. The previous few months since that fall had been stressful while things were out of balance, so this weekend was a time when I hoped to be spiritually refreshed and gain my breath once more.

My plan was to break my fast on Easter Sunday morning (it had not been intensive, but I still enjoyed tucking into fried bacon and eggs, orange juice, cornflakes with a generous sprinkling of sugar, and numerous other delicacies/treats), and then I planned to go to the Sunday-morning Easter service.

As the weekend progressed, I began questioning more and more whether I was on the right track ultimately. I knew that God had put me in dentistry, and then I had withdrawn due to my first relapse. There had been no direct leading that research was a new direction in my life. I had just naturally progressed into this following the interruption to my dental studies.

Now I began questioning (and praying about) whether I should be pursuing a degree in academia in the first place. I was beginning to have the idea form in my thinking that maybe this was just a pause where lessons could be learned before returning to my original degree. In fact, God was preparing me as to whether dentistry was even in my long-term future to begin with.

On this day, after cleaning up from breakfast, it was time to get going if I was going to make it to the church service. But I still needed to do the mundane chore of taking out the rubbish. To do so, I needed to visit my garbage bins below my front patio. I walked out my front door and looked up into the sky to find what I believe was a promise from God to me alone, as no one else would have seen it unless they were viewing it from my vantage point.

There was an even coverage of cloud across the sky, except for one area in the shape of a cross. I took it as a reminder to me that no matter what came across my path, Christ had gone before. He had paid the penalty, walked the path, and now was present with the Father, interceding for me, and the Spirit was always with me even when I did not see it at the time.

Returning to my original course of study may not make sense to anyone else, just as no one else would be able to see this formation in the clouds except me. In fact, it may not even make sense to even me, to follow directions back into a dental degree rather than academia. Put simply, it was time to push on and push through and trust Him.

A peace settled over me that what I was doing now, even though it was not what I had originally been led into, was where I should be for now. I did not know for how long or what was next, but they were issues for another day and another time. Like that old military saying, I had not received any new orders, so I should simply keep following those orders that I had already received. My responsibility at this point was a research degree, so I needed to focus on this, not on peripheral distractions in life. My future may not involve academia or even dentistry. New instructions would come when needed. But right now, just be patient and at peace where I was—and be faithful! Such was my Easter weekend of 1995. Another instance of God's hand.

Yet another source through which I have found God speaking to me and felt His hand on me was via those around me—mentors, friends, and the church body. In 1996, while involved in the Franklin Graham Festival, I met some men who were involved with Promise Keepers, Australia, as it was first kicking off here. While going along to a few of the meetings, I learned mentoring was big on their recommendations, so I decided to ask some older men who were going through their own health struggles to mentor me.

The first gentleman had terminal bowel cancer. I met with him for some ten months until he reached the end of his journey. The second gentleman suffered from aggressive rheumatoid arthritis, and we met for two years until I left that church upon getting married. I did touch base with him after he too was diagnosed with terminal cancer and visited with him in his final days.

Once I moved churches, it was a number of years before I began to meet with anyone again, but eventually, I approached a man who I had a lot of respect for. He was a retired church pastor, and I felt there was a lot that I could glean from him in my pursuit to become more Christlike and in discerning how best God wanted to use me. And so we began to meet regularly. While he was not struggling with ill health when we first began to meet, he did eventually suffer severe health concerns and the normal struggles of aging.

All of these men were men of God and were able to share with me both wisdom and insight. They all assisted in developing my outlook on life while living with a chronic disease. They also helped me to figure out my questions and philosophy on suffering from a Christian point of view. At the very least, they each helped to put a new perspective on the whole dilemma because all of them at one time or another had gone through the issue of life being hindered and held back by health yet ran their race well. Two of them actually passed through "the valley of the shadow of death" (Psa 23:4 KJV). I was able to meet with them right up to nearly the end of their journey here on earth. This also helped prepare me in my understanding, comfort, and peace for when my father died of cancer years later.

After salvation, what is next for the Christian? According to John Stott, that step in our Christian walk is to become Christlike. I would also term this as intimacy with God. I have heard it described that we first receive salvation, and then we grow via discipleship before becoming "sent ones" to start the whole process again. And this is what I found myself being encouraged and spurred along to do in these mentoring relationships. God spoke to me through these men even in their hindered abilities.

Other tools He used were those people around me who I would regard as friends to speak into my life, to share words of wisdom and encouragement in my walk of restoration. While I had had significant breakdowns in my personal life, there were numerous wise people who spoke into it. One such instance of this occurred shortly after my rural exploits when I received a surprise to encourage me greatly.

A letter arrived in the mail one day from a past lecturer who had taught me in my second year of university. He apologized deeply for not realizing the psychological anguish that I was going through at the time. He prided himself on being able to discern the mental state of his student body and to detect when someone may need that extra bit of emotional support. But he confessed, "I can't believe you sat there in the second row, week after week and I did not even suspect what you were going through. I'm sorry!"

I subsequently formed a close friendship, not only between the two of us but also with his family. As a brother in Christ, we spent some special times just talking life, exchanging spiritual insights, and sharing about the amazing way in which God can work in one's life. He encouraged me that God could still use me as I was.

And apart from times when members of God's own body (our church family) spoke into my life, giving me deep encouragement to keep going, there were also times when someone shared a simple Bible passage with me, or someone else presented me with a box of homewares (see "Congratulations", chapter 6).

There have been times when genuine love was expressed as people gathered around to pray for my healing (see "Healing", next chapter). In all of these cases, I saw the physical expression of God's hands in many ways, and it was exactly as it is with God's grace—something undeserved, which we can never hope to repay, even if we dream of doing so.

19

Healing

Patience is being happy
to wait for God to move
in His time as He chooses.

The gift of healing is one example where I have been persistent in petitioning God despite not receiving a 'Yes'. There have still been lessons learned (glorifying God), principles embraced (waiting), and assurances received ("My grace is sufficient for you"), but I remain as that widow, persistently seeking justice (in my case, healing). I continue to petition the Judge, but so far, I have not received the answer I am seeking. However, I am content and satisfied. God's ways are not my ways, and I must say, "That's okay!"

Glorify Me

Years ago, shortly after I suffered my first relapse, which forced an interlude to my study, I went to a weekend seminar at my then church on healing. During the seminar, we looked at how God had healed in Bible times, how He heals now, barriers to healing, and many other aspects of this issue that people grapple with. It was basically a comprehensive study on healing—what it is, what it means, what it does and does not entail, and when/how we should seek it.

It was a chance to go deeper with the whole concept of healing. The Bible records numerous instances of God healing people. And I actually learned about healing in a much deeper way than I had ever known it before. The weekend culminated in a service where healing was sought. It was a time when those close to you gathered around and prayed for you; hands were laid on me, and God was asked to send healing.

I remember sitting there, and when the prayers ended, I went to stand, expecting my legs to feel normal as I stood up out of my wheelchair, miraculously healed. But when I went to stand, there was nothing. Nothing happened. I felt nothing. But wasn't God supposed to heal if we had faith and asked? This brought on the question in my mind as to whether I would ever be healed or whether I would be this way for life. Regardless of whether I was healed or whether I would stay this way, how would I respond? How *should* I respond? And so began my education in how with healing, there are both miracles and mysteries. Why are some people healed at times, yet others are not?

It was about this time that I came across the story of David Roever,[26 & 27] who had been seriously wounded during the Vietnam War when a white phosphorus grenade detonated beside his head, taking half his face and multiple fingers off and leaving him with extensive permanent scarring. His testimony impacted me greatly, and as I remembered Bible characters such as Paul and personal testimonies such as Joni Eareckson Tada, I began to wonder whether maybe God would use me in my current state *with* my scars (disability) and that this could be more powerful than having a testimony of healing.

It was at this time that I realized that I not only held a testimony to those around me but that I was also surrounded by "a great cloud of witnesses," as we are told in Hebrews 12:1a. They saw my every action, so I could glorify Him before onlookers both seen and unseen by having an uncomplaining and patient attitude. This being despite whatever my physical circumstances and condition might be. As I processed these feelings and questions, God worked on me to teach and instruct me. I distinctly got the message from God, "Glorify Me".

As much as I wanted to glorify God, I also wished that I could turn back time ten years when I had never seen or heard of MS. It would have been so much easier not to have this disease in the first place. Despite this, I have never been angry at God, and I have not asked, "Why?" It was really more a question of "How should I respond?" And the question of "What now?" became my prayer—that God would find a way to use my story to glorify Him, if that was in fact what He wanted. I began to apply the concept that our purpose on this earth is primarily to bring God glory before seen and unseen realms; everything else is secondary to this. I was at peace with the fact that one day God may grant me healing. But this was my secondary desire and focus. My primary focus was to glorify God.

Wait

Years later, I found that the church that I attended after I got married provided much strength and support to help me in my journey as I endeavored to bring Him glory while I waited for healing, if it was coming at all. I had already come to a point of peace that it was okay if God wanted to use me in my frail, disabled state, as opposed to being healed, if this would bring Him more glory. I was able to edify and encourage those around me as I led by example—to give thanks in all circumstances. But that was not all. As well as giving it, I received encouragement.

My church family is integral to my mental and spiritual well-being and support. Those people who say, "I don't need to be part of a church", miss out on so much. That is why Paul warns about "not giving up meeting together" (Heb 10:25). One example of this came one Sunday morning following our church service. In part, the message had been about committing oneself for God to use as and where He wished, in whatever state we were. At that time, I was nearing the end of my initial term on the church council (see "Voice of God", chapter 16) and felt compelled to go forward at the conclusion of the service to offer my life anew to be used as He wanted. So, during the altar call, I asked Adrienne if she would join me at the front of the church in a prayer of rededication.

When we sat down at the front, I talked with her for a short time before we began praying. Then I was moved deeply when I felt one hand after another being laid on my shoulders as I prayed. As I finished my prayer, I came to the realization that people had spontaneously gotten up out of their chairs from all over the church, come down to the front, and gathered around us to pray for my healing. This was not why I had gone down to the front, but this act of love left me speechless.

A short time before, a Prayer for Healing ministry had been initiated, and Adrienne and I talked about going along but had been unsuccessful in fitting it within our busy schedule. As the group prayed for me on this morning, I asked myself, What is the difference between a Thursday morning and now? – Nothing! So, I joined with them as they petitioned God for my healing. At the end, I went to uncross my legs to stand up, but once more, just as years before at the healing conference, there was nothing.

But unlike when my initial request was denied years before, I found my identity in Christ as a child of God, and this stopped me from mourning my frail body and disability. For some, their identity comes from things such as their qualifications, job, and family. I learned that my identity is not found in these things. It is in Christ, and there is no better place to find it. One thing was obvious, as it had been years before at that conference: it was not going to be instantaneous healing. But that was okay! Who is to say how and when God will act? Maybe it would be gradual. I felt that I just had to be faithful and patient and wait, allowing Him to use me in whatever state I was in the meantime.

This was the day that we returned home from church and watched the movie *Facing the Giants* for the first time (see "Satisfied", chapter 15) only to be reminded that we needed to praise Him, regardless of our lot in life! This not only included issues such as pregnancy and children, which we were grappling with, but also the issue of healing. And as we were facing all of these issues at the time, this just added to the poignancy for us.

After my prayer for healing on that Sunday, I went to my physio appointment the next day. As part of it, I would practice my standing. My aim at the time was to strengthen myself for a possible/hopeful pregnancy. The best I had been able to do since 2004 was one minute. This day I stood four times; once for thirty-five seconds, then one minute. When it came to the third time, the physio aid said, "That's a minute. Okay, you can sit down". I replied, "No, I'm staying up", and remained standing for two minutes (praying and thanking God the entire time, just as I had learned from Jordan Rubin in times past when I had been asked to join the Church Council—see "Voice of God", chapter 17). I then repeated another stand for two minutes.

The next week, I was able to repeat these times, standing twice for four minutes each time. At the three-minute mark, the physiotherapist walked out from the office with the phone to her ear and a quizzical look on her face. I just looked over and smiled. She turned around, shrugged her shoulders, and walked back with a confused look on her face. At the end, the aide asked what was going on. But due to an unknown pregnancy result, I was unable to elaborate much at the time, except to say, "We are seeing God do some amazing things at the moment." Then, when it came to the third week, I stood for six, 1:30 and one minute respectively. We would see God move both as far as pregnancy results (Matthew) (see "Satisfied", chapter 15) and avenues for healing when He led us to embark on a course of nontraditional treatment (see "Stepping Out", next chapter).

As time went by though, I did end up losing more and more strength until I could not support my own weight. But we were still reminded that without Him we can do nothing! And that with Him, all things are possible. It is reassuring to know that God does not call the equipped; He equips the called! Especially encouraging for an oversized paperweight!

Shortly after that series of stands though, I received several phone calls early in the morning to report to me that the caller had dreamt of seeing me walking. I did not know what to make of this until I remembered how I had had dreams where I was walking also. I began to believe that, yes, one day God *would* in fact heal me. He would put that brick of healing in place. When, I do not know, and I do not need to know, because God is sovereign. God can do what seems impossible to us whenever He wants. I am convinced of this and have faith. But there is still the mystery. Maybe it will be the final brick in my life, and this makes it much easier for me to wait patiently. I am happy and at peace with however long it takes. God's timetable is not necessarily ours. My place is to wait and take the opportunities placed before me to glorify Him while I trust God to act when and how He so chooses.

Please forgive a small sidetrack to present the current situation at the time of publishing. Ten years previously, the physio that I was seeing at the time said to me regarding the use of a motorized bike, that since I was no longer able to support my own weight and stand, I probably could not pedal the bike so there was little benefit if any for me, so what was the point? As you may have observed, I don't like the phrase, "What's the point?" Whether it be in high school striving for a 990 TE score, trying to address water flow issues, dental studies, or pedaling a bike.

I told them to tie my feet to a motorized bike and we would see what might happen. On turning it on, the motor pedaled for me for one minute, and then we switched it over to active mode where I had to pedal. My right leg straightened out and then relaxed before my left leg straightened and then relaxed. They kept this up, alternating, and before I knew it, I was pedaling.

I have now been able to increase this to being able to pedal for half an hour. I can't stand, but I can pedal for 3.5 km from my wheelchair. God can do "immeasurably more than all we ask or imagine" (Eph 3:20)-that is the point!

After that time of prayer, I was not fully healed. I still had MS. But God had assured me that, with Him, "all things are possible" (Mat 19:26b). And this included being able to support and help Adrienne through any pregnancy that we may be blessed with. As far as healing went, I got the message: I just had to wait and glorify Him while I did.

My Grace Is Sufficient

In the following months, my health plateaued, and I saw no great signs of healing. It was like I had been on a mountaintop and then descended to a mountain saddle that became a ridge along which I continued my journey. To where it would lead, I had no idea, but I knew the One who did!

One day while I was trying to perform a lateral transfer, I fell out of my wheelchair. And as I lay spread out on the floor, I remembered how it had been a few months prior when I had been amazed. Things had been different. After my last request for healing, I received a strong feeling that I needed to continue to be patient and wait.

I had seen improvement, but why had it stopped? As I was asking myself this question, the words, "My grace is sufficient for you, for my power is made perfect in weakness" (2 Cor 12:9a) came to mind. A gentle reminder from God through scripture that I had to rely on Him whether there was healing or not. To praise Him whether we win or lose, whatever our lot in life. And I would have an opportunity to do just this shortly.

In September 2011, we finally acted on a leading that we first had when Adrienne was pregnant with Matthew. Yes, we had seen some mighty works while Adrienne was pregnant, as well as shortly after Matthew was born. God had sustained me during her pregnancy so that the demands of caring for me intensively were greatly reduced. This was evidenced when I saw increased strength in standing as well as in numerous other fulfilled promises along the way. Once Matthew's birth was behind us, we were able to refocus on the issue of healing. It would be a chance to see just how sufficient His grace was.

Following the birth, we found that I required an increased level of care. Together with the normal increased level of commitment and demands involved with a newborn baby, we had not been able to attend the weekly Prayer for Healing ministry held at our church. So when I shared this fact with the convener for prayer, he suggested we follow what is instructed in James 5:14, and "call the elders of the church to pray". This is what we did. Leaders, pastors, and elders of our church gathered one evening to lay hands on me, pray over me, and anoint me.

My hope had been that there would be either instantaneous healing or at least rapid improvement. I had done my part being patient. Now it was God's turn to reward that patience with healing, right? I was once more mildly perplexed when nothing happened. Had I misinterpreted or misheard what we had been instructed by God? Every time I seemed to seek healing, my expectations rose as I pictured myself being fully healed immediately. But each time I did not see immediate healing, the same questions rose in my mind. Had my own desires and expectations clouded what He had been trying to tell us? As I went to Him now, I found that my heart was put at rest as I was reminded what came immediately before when Paul was promised sufficient grace in 2 Corinthians 12. Paul had asked for the thorn in his flesh to be removed three times.

I laughed to myself, as it seemed like I had approached God three times just as Paul had done. And it was as if I got three separate answers in return. The first time, His reply was, "First things first. Glorify Me". The second time I sought healing, I received a gentle, "Wait". And the third time, it was almost as if He sighed, "Enough already! My grace is sufficient for you—remember!" Over the years, I have been reassured that my place was to wait. Wait and let God move when and how He wants so that He alone will be glorified, and until then, His grace is sufficient. Sometimes we are slow learners, but it is true. I have found Him fully sufficient!

God's delays do not mean God's denials. He has His plans for us, but He also has His timetable. When we petition God without receiving an obvious answer, our patience and testimony can still bring glory to Him. In my case, as people see me waiting patiently despite suffering, they see me testify that God is in fact real. Often in modern-day Western Christian thought, God's faithfulness is misunderstood as being something that should remove suffering from our experience immediately on demand. Prosperity doctrine has played a role in promoting this wrong theology and misunderstanding. At times, suffering may be removed, but I have found that when suffering remains, God has not been unfaithful or unloving. There are many examples in scripture of people who were greatly loved by God yet who suffered. Paul, Mary, Martha, Lazarus, and Job to name just a few, and the ultimate example—that of Jesus Christ. All of these examples stand as monuments to glorify God.

I still dream, like the character Jimmy in one of Steven Curtis Chapman's songs called "That's Paradise"[28], of that place where everything will be made new (including frail bodies) and there is no longer any need for God to provide our needs. In the meantime, I have found God has used me with my disability. This was not dependent on healing of any kind. In fact, I was asked to write an article for a Christian medical magazine, which gave me an opportunity to encourage and edify a wider Christian audience.

I wrote:

Even though I have sought healing repeatedly since I was struck down with MS, I have not received miraculous healing, I have not received progressive healing through either traditional or alternate medical treatments. Instead, *through spiritual healing* my thinking is now, 'Whatever You want Lord.' I have found that one of my favorite verses in the Bible is so true!

> Be anxious for nothing, but in everything by prayer and supplication, with thanksgiving, let your requests be made known to God; and the peace of God, which surpasses all understanding, will guard your hearts and minds through Christ Jesus. (Phil 4:6–7)

We (and I include myself in this) must allow God room to work in unexplained and sometimes unexpected ways including delays or *to receive* the answer 'Wait'. Sometimes we (and I have… been guilty of this) focus on having no harm done in medical treatments (or risking no detrimental effects) that we pursue results at the expense of ethical process. Or we do not pursue them at all. We say, 'What worked for someone else should work for me' regardless of how it was sourced. Or we can expect results from God on demand. With the only acceptable result *as far as we are concerned* being 'Yes'. Then we try to understand how and why things do not happen the way we think they should. When we do any of these things, we hamstring God from being able to do what He does best. Work despite us - when and as He so desires! [Italics added.][29]

It was an opportunity to share numerous lessons learned during my journey with MS over more than half a lifetime. I found that He opened the way for me to share some of my knowledge and experience with others, to encourage and strengthen them in their own faith walk. I can also say that I do not know how or where treatment and healing will come from, but my strength and perseverance come from Christ, and I will hold onto Him.

Like Paul, I received three answers over the years when I sought healing. I have come to a point where I understand that it is a matter of me waiting on God. When He so desires to put that final brick in place (and who is to say that that will be the final brick), then and only then will I be healed, and I can honestly say, "That's okay with me!" His ways are not our ways. So who am I to say when and how He will answer my appeal? Until then, there is work to do. I hope in some way people may see something of God's greatness so that I may advance the gospel, similar to Paul but in my own way. In the meantime, His grace is sufficient, and I have found that there are still benefits along the way.

My house is in the process of being rebuilt (psychologically, spiritually, and emotionally). In fact, I feel that my house is more than being renewed. And at the same time, it is falling down (physically) because we all live in a broken world, of which I am a part. But I am fully aware that I will not need this body for much longer, so I know that just as Stuart Hamblin observed in his famous song, "This Ole House"[30] I don't have time to fix the roof, floor, doors, or windows because there are more important things to focus on until I vacate the premises (either by death or rapture).

So far, I have not received healing. Whenever I have asked for it, the answer, among others, has been, "Not yet" but as I once heard Joni Eareckson Tada point out when she reflected on a prayer to Jesus in her address at the National Religious Broadcasters (NRB) Convention, 2013:

> A 'No' answer to a request to be physically healed, has meant 'Yes' to a deeper faith of You, meant 'Yes' to a deeper prayer life, 'Yes' to a greater understanding of your word, and has purged sin from my life, and forced me to repent on your grace, and increase my compassion for others who hurt, to put complaining behind me, and hope, and given me a life of freedom, and trusting in You. What an excitement about heaven! It has pushed me to give thanks in times of sorrow … and helped me preach my faith, and helped me to love You more Jesus … You did not give me the physical healing I want but the deeper healing.[31]

And likewise, with this knowledge, He has also brought an unshakable perfect peace to my heart.

So, just like there was silence during our journey as far as the IVF process went, there was also silence when it came to a positive answer to requesting healing. We eventually received an answer when it came to our IVF question, but so far there is still no answer when it comes to healing. I am certain of God's goodness in His ultimate plan in these matters. We only see a small part of the picture. We may see a 5 x 6-inch photo-sized area. And what's more, it may be like a tapestry and may only be seen from the rear, with all the knots, but God sees the whole 8 x 6-foot wall hanging from the front. We are commanded to be persistent in our petitions whether we see any answers or not—to endure patiently. So I was not doing anything wrong in repeatedly seeking healing. God commands us to continually seek (like the woman who persisted looking for justice). Even when the hard times came, I found that He was both faithful and sufficient to provide my needs and use me despite my frailties and so glorify Himself. I can say that I have learned to rely and wait on God, but I will still continue to knock on the door. I will either be healed, or I will walk through it at the end of my marathon.

In this life, there are many questions, unanswered queries, and just as many loose ends. But even if healing does not come here on earth, it will not be long till I'll be in a better house! The answers will be known, loose ends tied off, and I will see the full picture as it should be viewed. And that is even better than physical healing. Deeper healing is better by far. And in the meantime, we are called to wait as we glorify and praise Him.

20

Stepping Out

Thank God for what you have.
Trust God for what you need.

Shortly after the time of prayer with our church leadership in our lounge room, we were watching a science program called *Catalyst* on television, and there was a story on MS. This chapter is about how we stepped out in faith and received God's faithfulness in return. Only a few weeks earlier, I had been speaking with a doctor about possibly going on a six-month course of antibiotics to help get on top of a series of UTIs that I had been suffering. The treatment as described by the *Catalyst* program did not sound like much of an extension (eighteen months as opposed to six), and the more I looked into the underlying principles and rationale behind this alternate treatment, the more it sounded both logical and feasible.

We decided to approach our GP regarding this left field treatment to discuss details in depth and the possibility of stepping out and commencing this treatment if there was agreement that it could be beneficial. We still had a few questions that we wanted to put to him. Were there any downsides/dangers we were overlooking? Would he be prepared to prescribe the required antibiotics? He made sure we understood what we were asking but then surprised us by saying, "Let's do it!" We were amazed that after talking about the relevant issues (high expense and possible antibiotic resistance), there was no real objection. We felt that this was confirmation that it was worth pursuing this course of treatment.

We returned home with confidence, and then four hours later there was a knock on the door. It was someone we had met with a year earlier. After following some advice we had given to them, they had saved a substantial amount of money. Now they handed us an envelope and told us that it was a love gift to show their appreciation. We thought there had been confirmation earlier in the day, but now this was not just confirmation, it was affirmation! It was time to step out in faith and see just where God would take this treatment that was unrecognized by mainstream medicine but potentially could be used for full or partial healing. We did not know how He would use it, but we knew that in all things He was in control, was good, and was sovereign.

Two days later, I sourced the relevant supplementary drugs, and at the end, I calculated how much they would cost. The total came to just below the love gift that we had received. He had provided! But this was not to be the only example of His provision. In fact, during the course of the treatment, we would see it in numerous and varied ways. As we stepped out, we would see God's affirmation repeatedly.

Less than a week later, we celebrated my brother-in-law's birthday at a restaurant. Partway through the meal, the waitress came to our table and said, "Do you remember the gentleman who was sitting on his own at the table over there? Well, he just paid for his meal, but he also left money with us to pay for your meal also, so please, enjoy." He paid it forward, as this blessing is sometimes referred to.

Shortly following this, we attended the Queensland MS Society Conference and their Annual General Meeting. When we arrived home, there was a message on our answering machine from my brother who was a pastor at a local church. Someone had sent a check for us but wanted to remain anonymous.

We did not know how much this check was for until he transferred the funds into our account. It was enough to pay for the initial setup for *all* of the medications (antibiotics *and* dietary supplements) all over once more.

Some of the antibiotics were meant as short-term courses only, so there was potential drama with the national health fund (PBS) if they were prescribed repeatedly for long periods. With these gifts, we were able to subsidize all medications needed rather than relying on PBS funds. Yes, God was good!

Jump forward a couple of weeks, and we received an unexpected gift once again. We were presented with a check to pay for a weekend away for Adrienne and myself as a way to bless us. Then, over Christmas, we received further gifts from different sources, to be used wherever we felt the need (we used them to subsidize medication). God continued to provide!

Again and again, we saw God provide financially to allow us to undertake this course of treatment. We did find over the duration of this treatment that it was beneficial, as the progression of the MS slowed and seemed to even have halted. Previous disability was not removed, but we saw a difference in the downward advance of the disease.

About six months into the treatment, I met with the doctor to give him an update. Talking about my progress, I said, "If A is total disability (where I was heading), and if B is full recovery/healing (about a meter away), I have turned around, and am 5 mm from A, slowly heading back toward B. I still have a long way to go, but at least I am heading in the right direction!"

The progress of my antibiotic treatment.

Put together, what did it all mean? There are three ways in which we see healing today. The first is immediate or miraculous healing where the condition suddenly disappears (often with prayer). The second is a progressive healing which has two aspects: seen either during traditional medical treatment (where a course of accepted medical treatment is undertaken over time—e.g. Utilizing radiotherapy, antibiotics, surgery, chemotherapy etc.) or by using alternate treatments that have not yet been proven by scientific method. As a result, many of these treatments have been dismissed despite being effective. But there is a third option where none of these categories of healing are seen. Times when God may say, 'No' or 'Wait' to our desires and prayers. At these times, He heals us in such a way that we can mentally or spiritually come to a point of acceptance. We express perseverance and can glorify God even more.

By the end of this course of treatment, we saw no dramatic healing or improvement. I had previously accepted that God's grace was sufficient and that the timing was entirely in God's hands. Once more, it seemed that there was going to be no dramatic, miraculous, or progressive healing as I saw it. So where to next? There are two lessons I learned during (what seemed like) those failed requests for healing.

Firstly, it is a matter of patience! We had done all we could and followed what we are commanded in scripture. God had heard our prayer and promised that even where we have faith as small as a mustard seed, we can move mountains, and our prayer will be answered in some way (yes, no, or wait). Currently, it was and has been 'Wait!' Since 1990, I have often reflected and commented that it seems like God on my invitation pulled down the jumble of a life I called a temple and house, which I had built in my youth. He then began to rebuild my life brick by brick. This is an ongoing process. I am yet to see a brick called healing. At the right time (God's perfect time), I know that this brick will be put in place. Until then, it is not the right time. All I can do is wait! Another way of looking at it is that His delay is not His denial. I know it *will* come one day!

In the meantime, while I wait, I am thankful because despite the hardships and pain, God has been able to build my life in the way that He wanted. And He certainly has been faithful all the way! I can honestly say, regardless of whether I am disabled, partly abled, or fully healed, I have my mandate—not to try to understand the full picture when I see only part of it. I know the artist who sees the whole picture and who in fact created it.

Secondly, despite MS being a degenerative neurological disease where the insulating material in the central nervous system (CNS) is attacked and lost, meaning that what abilities you lose are widely varied depending on what part of the CNS is affected, you may wonder how I cope with and handle the prospect that this condition will potentially get worse and become more disabling as time passes, especially when I feel that there has been no ethical or moral solution/treatment available to date. That means that in my future, I would inevitably become more of that human paperweight rather than accept these treatments! Another of my favorite verses reveals the secret:

> Listen, I tell you a mystery: We will not all sleep, but we will all be changed—in a flash, in the twinkling of an eye, at the last trumpet. For the trumpet will sound, the dead will be raised imperishable, and we will be changed.
> (1 Cor 15:51–52)

When God's purposes for my life are complete, I will join Him in heaven through death or rapture (whichever comes first). I will receive a perfect, whole body because, as we are promised, "He will wipe away every tear from their eyes. There will be no more death, or mourning, or crying, or pain, for the old order of things are passed away" (Rev 21:4). Things such as sickness, disability, infirmity, and all that is present in an imperfect world will be gone, including MS. I will be in heaven, which is all perfection. So, I am in a win-win situation of either being healed in this life or receiving final and perfect healing in the next. And if in fact there is no healing in this life, then when I reach glory, I will have the knowledge and understanding to answer all my questions that I may have had regarding delays. I will be satisfied completely. The answers will be infinitely sufficient.

I may have had to wait for it, but I will know the reason, and it will be more than acceptable! Although I doubt that reasons or explanations will mean much at that time. In fact, I think they will not matter that much at all. Where and when physical healing occurs is sort of irrelevant. Do not get me wrong. It would still be nice! But while I wait, what I need to do is to glorify God and offer myself to be used as best I can. And this means that if God can use me more powerfully in a healed state, of course, I will praise Him! But if God can use me more powerfully with MS in a wheelchair, I still will praise Him!

MS may not be a comfortable place in which to live, but God has given me comfort. I went through a period when I wondered whether I could or would even survive. This period seemed to go on and on. But once I did dealings with God to get my life straightened out, He gave me a peace that cannot be put into words.

I feel that I may have a disability for sixty to ninety years here on earth, and I am at peace with that because I am promised a perfect and imperishable body once I reach heaven (1 Cor 15:42–44). Until then, I have received at the very least spiritual healing where I am in a win-win situation! I will either receive healing in this life, after which God will be glorified, or I will receive ultimate healing and a new body when I reach glory. Which is better? I am also in a quandary about this, as in this physical state, I am getting to know God better, but my task is to not only know Him better but to make Him known and so, to glorify Him.

Looking back, I can say without hesitation that I am totally comfortable with my lot, even if it lasts for a lifetime. I may have had a certain set of dreams, but God had different plans. In the end, they were much better. I know He is there for me at all times. And as we are told in the Psalms, that "weeping may endure for a night, but joy comes in the morning" (Psa 30:5b), my night may last the entirety of my life, but I know that joy will come in the morning. And in the meantime, He will sustain me and provide in all things that I need.

Some people are so terrified or repulsed by disability and infirmity that they do not give the implications of medical treatments a second thought. If they cannot accept the prospect of a wheelchair or degrading health, then untested, risky, unethical, or even dangerous treatments may be undertaken despite doctors and family trying to help them come to terms with their future instead. The lessons I have learned have helped solidify where I stand on these issues. One such issue is that of embryonic stem cell treatments (ESCTs).

A lady by the name of Mary Jane Owen, who suffers a genetic anomaly that caused her to lose her sight, was mostly deaf and confined to a wheelchair. She spoke before a US Senate committee in the year 2000, echoing my feelings succinctly:

> We are involved in a frenzied pursuit based on fear ... We fear our own vulnerability ... We are terrified of disabilities, we are terrified of disease ... We do not cure our vulnerability because it exists, and, I would submit that it is a positive, not a negative ... Our fear, our frenzied fear, our dread, our abhorrence of our shared vulnerability is what drives this pursuit of some way to escape...We in contrast are created unique, separate from all else, we have gifts. We have weaknesses. My weaknesses, your weaknesses. My strengths, your strengths ... Those intertwined weavings create the strongest social fabric ... Do I want to see again? Do I want to hear as well as I used to? Do I want to dance again? I'll be okay, but please know that I do not want those things at the cost of any living person, and I consider live embryos to be 'people'.[32]

In light of this, what does it mean in a practical sense? As far as any potential treatments for my MS, it means we will not accept or cause the destruction and killing of innocent life (even when, as some may say, "it is at least giving a purpose to those embryos that would otherwise be discarded"). It means that we have resolved not to accept or administer any treatments for my MS unless we can first confirm that it has in no way utilized embryonic stem cell material. We have wrestled with this issue of stem cell research, (not 'should we or shouldn't we'). Instead, we have thought long and hard in learning about the process itself, about what it means for me.

Another thing that I am thankful to God for is that He helped me to complete my dental studies so that I was equipped to knowledgably weigh up and critically assess scientific research, advances, and treatment therapies. We have embarked on other nontraditional (as far as the wider medical world goes) treatments, including antibiotics and dietary supplements, improving diet according to biblical principles, and essential oils. I continue to give God the opportunity to act as far as healing goes, but ultimately, healing will always come from God Himself.

I am once more reminded of the song that Steven Curtis Chapman released in 1992 on his *The Great Adventure* album called "That's Paradise,"[33] telling the story of a man named Jimmy who spent every day in a nursing home by his wife's side. In their decrepit state, he would read of the certainty that was theirs. And it would bring tears to their eyes as they dreamt of the time when the long night would end, all things would become new, and joy would never end. This song is closed by Chapman with a joyful statement that gives the song its title, "That's Paradise". This is my hope too! It has been interesting how I have found that frailty and disability have helped bring into focus my future dream of when healing will come and perfection follows. Stepping out was all worth it (for both physical and spiritual healing)!

21

Jehovah Jireh

He will supply
all of your needs.

Looking back, God was not only a provider as far as medical treatment went, as discussed in the previous chapter ("Stepping Out"), He was also Jehovah Jireh in many other ways—housing, motor vehicle, finance, study, and family life to name just a few.

Health

As detailed in the last chapter, God provided opportunity to pursue ethical treatment options (even if they have not yet been proven) and then provided financially to allow us to undertake that journey. I may not have seen full healing, but I feel that the simple fact that He provided for these endeavors was His blessing for taking the hard road and ensuring medical ethicality. It may not have been complete physical healing, but I did receive spiritual healing. He had a reason for taking us down this path even though we may not fully understand it yet. What we do know is that the progression of my MS has been greatly slowed/halted. And I have found that my faith has grown steadily as I accepted that if anything is to work, it will be by the hand of God—through His providence, provision, and goodness.

God showed Himself faithful, as He did earlier during our endeavors to fall pregnant. We had seen a real provision where the government increased its coverage through the medical system to support out-of-pocket medical expenses (which included IVF procedures). We are still amazed that this extra coverage became available just prior to embarking on our IVF journey, and the funding was ceased just after Matthew was born.

Housing

He had always provided rental properties for my accommodation over the years, but then He stepped it up another notch. In 2002, my wife and I decided to approach the Housing Commission about whether they would be willing to allow us to purchase the property in which we resided. I had received a disability-equipped house in 1997 in which to live (another provision as a single person), but after marriage, we wanted to begin a family, and this house was only a two-bedroom house—certainly not large enough for a family. The Housing Commission declined our request, so we knew that we would have to move if we wanted to start a family. We sat down and listed those features that we desired in a potential house and began a search.

Then one Friday, Adrienne had been down at Wynnum (a bayside suburb of Brisbane) visiting a client when she decided to stop in at a real estate agent's office to see what they had listed. They had nothing at the time, but they knew of a house that would be coming on the market the following week. We went and had a look at the house and within a few hours decided this was definitely a provision.

When we looked at our list, every item but one could be found in this house (and this feature could be easily rectified). The other amazing thing was that when you sell a house to make a profit, a standard practice to increase your return is to renovate the kitchen or the bathroom. The house we were looking at had neither of these renovations done, which kept the price down but also allowed us, without hesitation, regret, or guilt, to freely perform our own renovations to make these rooms disability friendly. We would have to gut these rooms, and it would save us from having to do so in a newly finished house. This was another massive provision! God had provided for our shelter.

Motor Vehicle

He also provided for our transport needs. In January 2012, my father-in-law rang. I could hear the excitement on the answering machine as he announced, "I just had to call." Adrienne picked up the telephone quickly to hear the rest of his enthusiastic message.

He had been out one day when he drove past a set of industrial sheds that had a large disability sign on it. Outside was a car with a lift extending out of the side door and what looked like a wheelchair sitting next to it. He went in to see what it was all about, only to be stunned when he walked through the door. Inside the shed were about twenty cars, all with electric lifts of different descriptions. Each had a car seat that converted into a wheelchair (electric or manual) or simply a fixed chair to lift the occupant up into the car. He inquired about the story behind the vehicles. And this was even more astounding.

In Japan, the government has a very generous subsidy plan for disabled people, whereby they can purchase new vehicles that have been built specifically for people, with their needs catered for. On top of this, there were two other considerations.

1) An emissions regulation resulted in increased registration costs after six to seven years.
2) The bank interest rate in Japan had dropped to an all-time low of 0.00 percent.

As a result, whenever the registration costs for cars rose, the default response was to buy a new car, and likewise, whenever people wanted to purchase a car, they would tend to buy a brand-new car rather than a used car. As a result, there was no secondhand car market to speak of in Japan. This businessman had recently completed all of the government compliance requirements in Australia to be able to import these secondhand vehicles.

The end result was vehicles that had been designed and built in the car factory back in Japan with an integrated wheelchair/car seat hoist incorporated into the vehicle at a much lower price than installing an after-sales add-on to a standard car in Australia. We had investigated purchasing a new vehicle about twelve months earlier but found that there were only two after-sales systems available in Australia at the time.

The first was where an electric hoist was mounted externally out in the weather on the rear of the vehicle. This meant you would be tied down in the rear of the vehicle after a significant amount of seating had been removed. It would cost in the vicinity of $40,000.

The second system was just beginning to appear on the market and consisted of a ramp at the rear of the vehicle with a sunken floor. But this would still require you to be tied down at the very rear of the vehicle. And all seats except two front seats had to be removed. This was a cheaper option but still cost between $20,000 and $30,000.

In both situations, it would require you to purchase a vehicle capable of accommodating a wheelchair (usually a van of some kind). It would be foolish to make such an investment on an old vehicle. So, to purchase a suitable vehicle new would cost around $70–80,000.

And so, to purchase a vehicle with either kind of system would cost between $90,000 and over $100,000, which was way out of our capability. The only way we could possibly afford such a suitable vehicle in years to come would be to purchase a secondhand modified vehicle (which usually came with a high odometer reading, was fairly old, and included significant wear and tear).

We noted that in the Japanese cars, the disabled individual was seated among the other passengers, not tied down in the rear like a piece of luggage, which was a real plus as far as maintaining one's dignity. Another advantage of this new system was that the hoist was protected inside the vehicle, not mounted outside on the rear of the vehicle. And only one or no seats needed to be removed in the design. And then, the factor that really brought this idea within our financial reach was that, because of the high government subsidy and their secondhand status, the price of these fully modified vehicles was usually less than one-third the price of purchasing and modifying a vehicle in Australia.

Adrienne and I agreed to go and view the cars the following Monday to hear about the whole system for ourselves and find out a bit more about how it all worked economically, but after just two hours, we looked at each other and whispered, "We *have* to do this." We both agreed that this was a God-thing! Then, when we went to examine our financial situation to see if we would be able to purchase one of these vehicles, we found that we were able to draw down sufficient funds from our home loan. The extra payments we had been able to make previously came to the exact amount required.

God had been our provider even before we realized there would be a need. Six months earlier, there had been an opportunity to purchase a narrow strip of land behind our property, which ended up falling through. We were disappointed at the time, but Adrienne reminded me that if we had purchased that land, we would have used the money in the home loan, and then these funds would not have been available to purchase the car.

This was an example of God working in ways that we cannot see or understand. Remember, "all things work together for good to those who love God" (Rom 8:28 NRSV), and we may not understand His plans because "His ways are not our ways" (Isa 55:8). But He was faithful, and yet again, He was our provider! Our Jehovah Jireh.

Financial

When I left home, no one really knew how hard I did it. I felt that if anyone knew the truth of the situation, I would be seen as a failure, and my low self-esteem and feelings of inadequacy would be confirmed. So I just could not bring myself to let on.

In those early days, there were times when I had nothing but a two-dollar coin in my pocket, with three days until I got my next student payment (I received a nominal allowance from the government), which would provide me with a small amount of cash. At those times, dinner would consist of an apple and a drink of water. I made excuses to my flat mate at the time that I was not hungry even though the smell of his dinner made me nauseous. I had to live extremely frugally, but looking back, I can say that God never let me down. He always provided in some way. Over the years, I have found Him faithful.

There was a promotional event run at McDonald's Toowong (on my way to the university) where you could buy a Big Mac burger for one dollar. Just after I received my fortnightly nominal student supplement, I felt flush with money and was able to afford seven Big Macs (which I thought was a bargain—seven days' worth of evening meals for a total of seven dollars). Then the second week would have to be those apples and water. I would deal with that when it came! Still, He did provide.

He provided for my needs when my flat mate moved out and I was left on my own. People were in fact inspired by God to provide for me, such as when I was given two boxes of kitchen crockery and utensils for when I would be left on my own. I would never have been able to buy those items myself, so God sent those people on His missions to help set me up for the future. They acted as His earthly angels.

Study And General Life

God provided for and sustained me in my study also. When life was turned upside down in a tangled mess, He came and met me in that mess. He spoke to me and upheld me when I felt like I was drowning and helped me to continue my education during this time. He sent the right person/song/scripture/book with the right message or the right act of love at just the right time.

When I attempted suicide, He protected me, nurtured me, and lifted me up from a very low point (the lowest point I have ever known). He did not let me go so that when I had the opportunity to share with a counselor, I was able to smile, shrug my shoulders, and say, "But you get that!" and then share my faith. Because God cared for me, He was and still is my provider.

When I saw how Doris van Stone had been approached by a child psychologist to point out the grace of God, I could see how my story had the potential to be used by God. Despite the chaos in which I had found myself, God had indeed been faithful in looking after me, physically, mentally, and emotionally, not letting me go. It has all been simply by the sheer grace of God.

When I returned to study, He guided my thought process to lead me to take action to seek reconciliation with my family when I heard that Insight for Living podcast. Again, God was faithful to give me courage to take the necessary steps. He did not let me go and was always by my side, prompting me so that I would have no regrets.

* * *

Further to these examples, time and again, I have found God providing for me. He provided for my mental health and stability, my physical and emotional needs, and my financial viability. After my life stabilized, I found that He also provided a partner to journey through my life with, children, a means for my shelter, transport, and medical needs. Throughout my life, He has faithfully provided in all areas.

At numerous times, there was no rhyme or reason as to why He did something until I found out later how it all fit together. Mind you, there are other things that to this day I still have not seen a reason for. In these circumstances, the assurance that I hold onto is that He can do "immeasurably more than all we ask or imagine" (Eph 3:20). Looking back, yes, His grace has protected me, provided for me, calmed and comforted me, restored me, and brought me through, and it will take me on. So, even when we do not understand, we can be sure that "all things work together for good" (Rom 8:28 NRSV).

Even when we do not deserve it, He chooses to bless us. It truly is a case of the grace of God. Yes, we have a good God. So I find that I want to trust Him even when I do not understand. One day I know everything will be made new (including frail bodies), and there will no longer be any need for God to provide where we lack, for Him to be Jehovah Jireh, our provider.

22

That's Okay!

*When you pray, lay out
your petitions before God,
and then say, "You Choose".*
—DL Moody

There are many things that have brought me to this point. Many were not very pleasant. I do not want or need to go through them again, because it is through them that I learned many things. It all seemed to start shortly after I prayed, asking God to clean my life out. He allowed my house of cards to fall. And in the end, it's okay!

As Christians, our self-worth should come from Christ and not from what we can offer to God (who we are or what we can do) or the moments when we feel close to God. It comes from grace entirely. When grace is received. When God reaches down to us in all our unworthiness to take us in His hand and carry us when we cannot walk. Even when we don't deserve it. We simply have to accept it.

The good news is Jesus Christ. It is not what He can do *for* you (being a yes-man for the list of needs we present in our prayers/wishes/demands), and it is certainly not obtained by *doing* certain things and not doing others for Him. It is what He has already accomplished in His death and resurrection. It is what He has done for us all. The divine Son of God came and took human form and died a human death as the payment for our sin. He died in the place of human sinners, before rising again from the dead for the salvation of every human being who would believe in Him, confessing Him as their Savior and Lord. He achieved it once and for all. A finished victory, where he took our place, paid the penalty of sin, and reconciled lost people to His father, God.

It was not until I fully grasped this concept that I was able to say, "That's okay".

"Nowadays, I can confidently say that my original neurologist without realizing it, summed it up perfectly when he said, 'Congratulations'. Because I have had the opportunity to take a front row seat to see a sovereign God at work."

And, in the same way, when I wrote that song and entitled it, 'Take Hold', without knowing it I wrote a preview to describe my eventual and current attitude – to take hold of every moment that I come across because it may be my 'last chance'. My last chance to drive a car, my last chance to take a walk, my last chance to cook a meal, my last chance to… I may never know when something may be the last time I do something but I know that one day all these lost abilities will be restored. And, 'That's Okay'.

Something I am glad to have seen within my lifetime came almost ten years after first meeting Adrienne. My thinking was straightened out, and I realized she was the one for me. It very nearly did not happen. At one stage, I was quite happy to remain single, but God's providential plan kept our paths crossing again and again until I caught up with His program. Sometimes I can be overly cautious, overly slow, and basically thick. But it was pretty hard not to get the message when God prompted Adrienne to make that first move.

There may have been times when I was overly slow and cautious, but there were other times after I had caught up with God's program when I was impulsive and acted without thinking. At these times, thankfully, God can and did still work despite me falling over myself, as I did when I finally proposed to Adrienne. Better late than never!

There have been similar times throughout my life when I have found He held me securely in His hand, and I saw that He is not a god who is absent or silent. He is a God who is there with us all the way. Yes, I certainly needed to receive confirmation when it came to marriage, but there were other times when I found that I heard Him in circumstances, messages, or that still small voice, so long as I listened and paid attention. Sometimes I found it in a booming voice that I could not miss. But there were other times when it was more difficult to hear that voice and understand what His directions were. In these times, I had to slow down so that I would not be distracted by the surrounding noise of general life. At first, this happened in a small, empty granny flat when I heard God reply to the cry of my heart one night, "You Are Mine". Then it came while serving within the local church and again during our IVF journey. At other times, it meant putting a pause to my study or taking a weekend to refocus.

My wife and I, despite eventually being amazingly blessed with two wonderful children, went through periods of silence when for a long time it seemed like we would have only one child. We kept knocking on the door, but there was only silence. Yes, we learned lessons, but why it took so long I do not know. It may be easy to say afterward but not so easy during those times. We found that He was always faithful, providing words of encouragement, scripture, and reminders of biblical truths in songs, books, and sermons. We remained in His hands.

Sometimes I heard His words in joyous times. It also came during times when all I could do was hang on and let God do the walking. He carried me. It may have been hard at times to go through some things, but in hindsight, I can truly say with Paul that "all things work together for good" (Rom 8:28 NRSV). As time went by, I was able to hear how God wanted me to reroute my life and to listen for and obey His voice. I began to live by the principle that if God said it, it was time for me to do it. No questions, no arguments. And it became easier to hear His voice when He spoke, and to discern His will.

So, God spoke and worked, I joined the program, and looking back, whether it be marriage or children, I can say, "That's okay!" It took several years for me to allow the truth that my identity was to be found in Christ alone to take root in my life. I had given my life to God, and He had told me, "You Are Mine". And this radically changed how I dealt with life in general. Before this, I had done Sunday School, I had done church band, I had done church every Sunday, I had done Bible study and increased my knowledge of the Bible. But then I realized that what I needed was not to do but to be. Now, if I have MS and this prevents me from *doing* anything, this no longer concerns me, because my identity comes in who I *am*, not in what I can or cannot *do*. He holds me in His hand.

I found that all I need is to trust in Jesus alone and not in what I can do. I do not simply do this for the benefits of salvation in the here and now (what you can get out of it in the short term). Over my lifetime, He has always been there, just like the Southern Cross obscured by clouds, and it was not until a bush bash that the truth of being His fully infiltrated my psyche, such that my self-image, purpose in life, and peace became totally secure in the fact that I am loved and desired by God. He gave everything for me, and I fully came to take hold of this fact during my rural exploits. I learned that I had always been in the security of His hand. Today, I have a close and personal relationship with Christ. I am His, and He is mine. And it is no longer just a pretty facade that I have to keep up.

Even if there is silence, we can know that He is still there. If we base it on emotions and whether we feel close to God, there will surely come times when our emotions tell us that God is not present or does not exist. It is like that partially visible Southern Cross. We have to simply accept what we know for a fact, regardless of how things seem or how we feel. In other words, it is faith.

So, "That's okay."

He led me back to complete my dental studies. At times such as this, I just had to push on, even in the silence. It ended up taking a total of nine years. Why? I don't fully understand, but I needed faith to accept the grace shown in being able to complete this degree. I have never actually practiced in this profession, but it did help equip me to assess scientific advancements and determine how I felt about potential treatments as a Christian.

Understanding my identity ultimately influenced how I viewed disability, infirmity, differences, and other hardships I encountered in life once I fully accepted God's grace. The impairments did not seem to matter as much anymore. It even helped me to trust God when circumstances did not make sense, regardless of whether I understood the why or not.

I do not begrudge my MS. Instead (as Paul says in 2 Corinthians 12:10 NRSV), "Therefore I am content with weaknesses, insults, hardships … for whenever I am weak, then I am strong." He has shown Himself faithful even in silence, so I can trust Him in every circumstance. As Joni Eareckson Tada says, "My weakness was not something to mitigate, or sweep under the carpet or hide from others, or be embarrassed about, or fail to admit. My weakness was something to own. Indeed, the Bible says to boast in because when we are weak, then he is strong."[31]

So, in the end, I can say, "That's okay."

Isaiah 61:4–8 talks about rebuilding, restoration, renewal, and reward. In my twenties, the white-ant-ridden beach shack that I called a temple in my youth was pulled apart. As far as physical health and healing goes, complete rebuilding may only happen once my life here on earth is finished.

There is an old chorus called Spirit of the Living God.[34] I have heard a variation that described my life well, with lyrics saying the following:

> Spirit of the living God
> fall afresh on me
> Break me, melt me,
> mold me, use me
> Spirit of the living God
> fall afresh on me.

After my life had been restored, I found that my passion became renewal. I know that reward will come once the rebuilding is finally finished. And I know it will be in God's sovereign time. This is where I am currently at in my Christian walk. In the years when my life was broken, melted, and molded, God was still faithful. So, I can actually say that I am thankful because, despite the hardships and pain, God was eventually able to build my life in the way that He wanted! It was painful, and it hurt at times, but He took something that was a mess, broke it down into pieces, and then melted and molded it into what He wanted in the process of rebuilding it. Yes, part of the work He did was by using my disability.

I have observed that disabilities do not happen only to the unlucky few but take place for us all. We all face disability at some point in our lives. One definition of disabilities is that they are, "the normal, expected, anticipated, outcome of the risks and stressors of the living process."[33] We may face it before birth, in early life, during the height of our productive years, or in our twilight years. For me, it happened at the age of seventeen, and to date, I've lived over half of my life with MS. Why? I do not know. But I believe it was the beginning of that deconstruction phase.

My life was further deconstructed after I left home, until it was ready to be restored and rerouted. There is the principle of A-S-King in the Gospel of Luke (Luk 11:5–10) where we ask, seek, and knock for our heart's desires and needs. I have asked, I have sought, yet there has still been no healing. It is now time to knock, knock, knock. It closes by telling us to be persistent. This never-give-up attitude is what is encouraged seven chapters later in Luke 18 in the parable of the widow and the unjust judge.

It is not for me to say in what order or time frame things should occur.

I just need to be persistent. There is also the parallel principle of Christian growth whereby salvation comes first, followed by discipleship, and then finally you become a sent one. It is not for us to say, "Right, I'm ready to move on to the next step, so let's go!" This has been my journey as well. During those steps of salvation, discipleship, and total surrender, there needed to be a phase of deconstruction followed by rebuilding. And now, renewal is occurring, and I know that there is no better place to be. In fact, I have found God has used me with my limitations (you may say, despite them). He has commissioned and sent me, as all Christians have been, in the Great Commission by Jesus when he says, "Teaching them to obey everything I have commanded you" (Matt 28:20) in the Gospel of Matthew and to tell of His greatness, goodness, and faithfulness (not least of all what he did and achieved on that cross nearly two thousand years ago).

So, in the grand scheme of things, I can say, "That's okay by me."

Looking back over my life, I have seen God's faithfulness. I gave my life to God when I was fifteen years of age. I remember the heartfelt prayer I made after listening to that Keith Green song, "Rushing Wind" (see appendix 1), where I prayed for God to take my life and make it into what He would have it be.

Again, I think of comments made at that Franklin Graham training session that prompted a simple statement, "Be careful what you ask God for. He may just say, 'Yes!'" that sums up my life.

Back in those days, He heard my prayer and answered it affirmatively, permitting the MS to cross my path and join my journey through life as a traveling companion—at times, not necessarily a welcome one but still one that would teach me lessons nonetheless.

The life I pictured as a child is not the one I find myself in now. I am not a missionary doctor, I have not married a missionary nurse, I do not have three or four children, and I do not work in deepest, darkest Africa. But I can certainly testify that when He says, 'Yes', there is nothing better (even when it may not always seem like it at times). He also said, 'Yes' to a closer walk with Him, 'Yes' to using me to glorify Him, 'Yes' to a win-win situation. And 'Yes' to much more!

I remember from when I was still able to climb mountains that the course of my life had some similarities. It was as if while I climbed (choosing to take a more difficult route than necessary) to the summit, I would continue to climb toward what I thought was the summit during those tough times, and the gradient would eventually change, at which point the climbing would become easier for a period. But when that portion of the climb was complete, I would find that as I rose above that next ridge, the climb was not yet complete. So basically, I would finally make it to a ridgeline, only to find a whole new vista. There would be another whole section hidden above and beyond that crest. There was always more mountain to go. When you climb a mountain, you may look up and focus on what you think is the summit, only to reach the prominence of that shoulder and find it was only a crest and that there is still further to climb. But without downplaying the importance of God's role, He would always be there like a Sherpa and a guide.

I *would* eventually reach the summit, but in a successful spiritual life, there is always more beyond the ridgeline/prominence. I only really began climbing that spiritual mountain called life when I prayed to God at that high school camp in grade ten. Climbing a mountain, you do reach a summit, but as Paul puts it in 2 Corinthian 9:24, I began to run the race, and I needed to run it "in such a way as to get the prize" as I cross the finish line as I pass into eternity. The question is, how well will you climb the mountain or run the race?

Sometimes, we are made fit for Christ's use by being melted in the furnace of affliction and then remolded on what I once heard referred to as 'the conveyor belt of trial'. I have been a student of suffering and adversity in the school of Christian maturity. But another analogy is used in Jeremiah 18:3–4. The potter is not happy with the type of jar being made, so he begins again and remolds it into something that seems useful. As a result, he had "a vessel that he could trust."[34]

Looking back, I *can* say honestly that I am thankful for it all. Some people may ask, "Was it worth it?" And my answer would be more than just, "That's okay" because if I ever wanted to share in His joy, it was on His terms. What He did in my life to make things right so that I can share that joy is definitely okay with me! As a result, I would say, "Yes, a hundred times over!"

23

Manifesto

Principles for Life

Romans 8:28 (NRSV) tells us, "All things work together for good for those who love God, who are called according to his purpose." And now I can truly say that this *does* mean *all* things. The deconstruction, the academic achievements, the reconciliations, marriage, children, the provision and voice of God, and rebuilding of my life once it was handed to Him, and yes, even the MS! Both the good things and the bad things. The happy things and even the tough things. And so I used to answer the question, "How are you?" by saying, "I can't complain!" (Because what is there to complain about when you are His?) But I have a new saying, "It's all good!" I have learned the secret to contentment—that if there is anything that, if you do not receive it, will make you miserable, that thing is more important to you than God. This order of priority cannot coexist with contentment, so after some tough lessons, I learned to let nothing become that number one thing above God. And then if He remains number one, I can testify that contentment will follow naturally.

When salvation is first received, forgiveness for sins is received. It is called judicial forgiveness—a once-only event where the penalty for sin is paid for. Despite the specific circumstances surrounding salvation (making it easy or otherwise to take that step in the first place), sometimes along the way (because we are all sinners), there is still the need to be cleansed and purified. This will impede the process of sanctification and is where relational forgiveness is needed (to maintain relationship with God). Once more, as in marriage, the principle of short accounts becomes important.

Ideally, this is a daily process, but on occasions, one thing after another muddies the water, and before you know it (as in my case), climbing that mountain becomes all the more difficult, as you need to be cleansed and purified all over again. I have observed that He may then help you to climb that mountain. And in fact, He may assist when He "permits what he hates to accomplish that which he loves."[35] We know that "If we confess our sins, he who is faithful and just will forgive us our sins and cleanse us from all unrighteousness" (1 Jn 1:9 NRSV), which in itself does not preclude the hard times. He can use both good and bad times to bring about cleansing, and it was upon my invitation that He did just that. I have found that if we keep our eyes fixed on Jesus through those unpleasant times while He reroutes, and He remains number one, then after those muddied waters are cleaned up, contentment and peace remain.

As in my case, a reroute may at times come with a total rebuild, which may be hard, but it enables God to use you and work in your life in a way that is more than you would ever have dreamt of before. Like the verse which says, "Now to Him who is able to do immeasurably more than all we ask or imagine, according to his power that is at work within us" (Eph 3:20). That "power that is at work" can be reconstructive work. And since that initial cleanup job in my life is done, it is a matter of keeping short accounts with God so that the plot does not need to be cleared out as aggressively in the future, if at all. So, the past is all okay, but where does that leave the future?

God used both situations and circumstances to reroute my life and endeavors. And we know that when God reroutes a life, there is a better way ahead by definition. He will not leave a life that is surrendered to Him to wallow in the mud if in fact there is a better way to live. But before He could reroute my life, it needed to be deconstructed, pulled apart, and cleaned up. During this time of deconstruction and rerouting, God showed Himself to me and assured me that I am His! Something that naturally grew from this in my spirit, as we are told in Hebrews 12, is to ensure that my life glorifies God to both seen and unseen witnesses (and part of this, here in the physical world now, is to know God and make Him known). This is my goal now and in the future.

I have learned that one way I can do this here on earth is to follow Jesus in whatever He wants and become more Christlike, to demonstrate in some way the incomprehensible, unexplainable, awesome nature of God, which we can never fully understand as humans. The way that I conduct myself in the midst of my disability I hope will do just that to those around. But the irony of the situation is that the only way I will be able to *do* this can be summed up in the statement, "Christ in me", for Him to *be* in me. And when He is, He is more than enough to sustain me. In the words of Joni

Eareckson Tada, "I don't want to waste my sufferings. I want to do the kinds of things down here on earth, and live in the kind of way that expands my eternal estate. Not diminishes it or shrinks it or shrivels it because of a complaining spirit."[38]

You will find that suffering and glory are linked in a number of places in the Bible, and if these times are handled properly, I have heard it said that our sufferings can actually bring glory to God. If difficult circumstances and suffering do not lead to complete collapse of one's identity and beliefs, then the question may be prompted from those around, "What is the strength that holds it all together?" There is only one thing—God. And this is where that cloud of witnesses again comes into effect. They are not simply a crowd to spy on us and observe our behavior; they are also put on our path to encourage and strengthen us. To act as God's hands, which is contradictory to the prosperity doctrine that infers that God simply makes us happy, healthy, and prosperous. God actually works in spite of and uses suffering and pain in such a way that if we relate to them in the correct way, we will become wholly satisfied and at peace with our life. And this is what I find has come to me. Now, some may say that maybe it is having had MS for so long that I have become used to it, but I like to think that it is a confidence in and relationship with the one who can give me true contentment.

I have heard another way of looking at it, as described by Timothy Keller.[35] At some point in our lives, we may need to sing what is commonly known as an aria, a moment in operas where the main character emotes something indescribable. The moment when they make a critical change in their thinking and mental disposition. In real life, we may also have the opportunity to sing out something like an aria in our suffering, hardships, or circumstances. We may not necessarily want it to come our way, but the question remains, 'What are we going to do with the opportunity when it is given to us?' Will we sing an aria and glorify God when it happens, or won't we? That is reality. It is a matter of *when* rather than *if* we will receive that opportunity to glorify God through suffering or disability, because it will come to us all at some point. In my case, if I do this well, I will hear Him say, "Well done" (Mat 25:21).

I have also heard it said, "As Christians, we believe that the variety in abilities and strengths, disabilities and weaknesses, in some mysterious way which we cannot fathom, reveals some essential part of our Heavenly Father."[36] Not only are we created to be unique, we are also created to be delicate. By God's wisdom, "We are fragile creatures, I don't think that is an error in our creator's planning."[37] And I have the privilege of demonstrating this fact in a practical way as I sing my aria. "That is not to say we do nothing to try to cure disability."[38] Should we flip the coin and, depending on what comes up (heads or tails), do anything to remove it? I believe not!

As I have said before, even while I live with a disability like MS here on earth, I live in a win-win situation. While this life may last for eighty or ninety years, it is only a speck in comparison to eternity. One day, I will be in eternity with my Savior (my primary desire), and a perfect body is just a derivative that comes as part of the deal. The focus is not on what we can gain, or even what He can do *for* us. In the meantime, here on earth (where I am just passing through), I have the promise that "My grace is sufficient for you" (2 Cor 12:9a). Nothing compares to His promise to be with me, and when I need Him, the reality of that presence keeps me going.

As far as I am concerned, heads or tails, I win! Whether I receive healing here in this life or live with a little discomfort and reduced ability, only to then receive healing in heaven, I have won the battle already because my identity is in Christ, I am His, and He is mine. I am secure in this. In the same way that I no longer need to chase achievement to feel that I am someone, I do not need to pursue whatever treatments I can get my hands on. And as such, I am reminded of another thing that I have heard, "How you handle your present depends on how you view your future, and what you do on earth will echo through eternity." Because I am His, I know that I will be with Him throughout eternity (which is the main thing), and this is when I will be able to run, walk, jump, dance, and do manual labor. (That is right; I am looking forward to doing some heavy labor in heaven!) I do not know whether we will sweat in heaven, but at least I will be able to work hard and enjoy it! Actually, I am looking forward to standing and singing praise at the top of my lungs! Something which with decreased lung capacity is near impossible currently. And so, my outlook on life and disability comes directly out of my spiritual identity. I know my future, so I can handle the present, knowing that one day I will receive an upgraded body.

Everyone in heaven will receive perfect bodies (which means that no one will have a better body than anyone else, as they will all be perfect). And this means that people with a disability or infirmity will receive that same upgraded body, but the upgrade by necessity will be to a greater extent. So, to help illustrate this, it is like an able-bodied person being upgraded from a family sedan to a high-powered luxury sports car like a Lamborghini.

A disabled person will upgrade to that same high-performance sports car. But it will be from a lower point, sort of like a push bike to that same Lamborghini. What an adrenaline rush that will be! So, if there is healing now, naturally it will be worth praise. But if there is not healing in this life, think about the eventual upgrade! Wow!

If there is no healing though, it is a dangerous mind-set to place assumptions on oneself by saying, "If I am not healed, then I have not prayed hard enough or I do not have enough faith", or to hold God to ransom by saying, "You mustn't love me!" Yes, someone may pray over/for me, and there may be legitimate healing, or something may happen in my body. Does that make me more favored by God than someone who is not healed? No! And vice versa. On the contrary. Instead, I identify with the comment, "God must have thought a lot of me to think that I could endure and handle this".

We live in a fallen, broken world, and as a result, everyone will experience hardship, pain, and ultimately death. For some of us, that pain means various degrees of sickness and disability that may even develop from thin air. For others, it may mean accidents may happen, resulting in injury, be it mental or physical. Any of these may even result in death (of loved ones or yourself). Or, it could also mean emotional pain as we go through the course of life. Even things such as lies, deceit, betrayal, and double-crossing can mark our life experiences. These episodes of misfortune touch all of our lives at one point or another.

And furthermore, we may or may not ever understand the why. Whatever has been lost or taken away throughout our lives will be replaced infinitely one day, and at that point, we will have full understanding and comprehension of the why's we had during our lives, and this will leave us fully satisfied in Him. These promises are only for those who are children of God. This book has been about my journey. Others may have a different story, but we can all be sure God is God, and we can trust Him. He has proven that He is indeed trustworthy. Even when we do not understand, we have to simply hold onto the fact (and not let go of it) that God is good for it!

Even when one is in less than full health, God is good! When we are sick, He is good! If, as in my case, there should be incomplete or no healing (yet!), He is no less good! If you are hurt by others, He is still good! When there is betrayal or disappointment, He is reliable and good! When on your deathbed, He remains perfectly good! The fact that we live in a fallen world does not make God any less good. Yes, God is good all the time, and all the time, God is good!

You may say this is a big call coming from someone who has had MS for more than half of his life and who has journeyed along this road. True, I have asked myself whether my trust of God is real. Am I deluding myself or promoting a false picture to other people? But I can assure you that it *is* real.

There are times in the past when I sought healing. Granting of my requests to this point has not come. I have pondered why God has not healed me. I know my deep psychological makeup. And maybe God knows that if I were to be healed, the focus may not be fully on Him. If there is one thing I do not want, it is for Him not to receive *all* the glory. And so it is okay with me if I do not see healing yet—if He will get more glory if I stay the way that I am; if He can use me more just as I am. In the words of Joni Eareckson Tada, "This also is okay, when I am forced to take a step down off the pedestal of pride, and accept the care which I would not otherwise need if it was not for my disability. It is a blessing, but it is a bruising of a blessing. It's a friend, but it's such a dark strange friend. And when others are doing your toileting routines [*among many other things*] … these things are so humiliating. But often, out of humiliation comes humility, if you allow humiliation to do its work" (italics added).[39]

If we make the most of the moment for His glory, not ours, it becomes, as she continues, a "reason why we all can boast in our affliction. Because our weakness has humiliated us. At times we end up looking foolish but then 1 Corinthians 15 assures us that, "It is the foolish things of this world that God has chosen to shame the wise." So, I need to make the best of it and boast in the Lord in that weakness. And I find that humiliation keeps me pretty humble."[40] At least I am learning this slowly.

I have also learned that God's silence does not mean God's denial. It may seem that He is silent, but He is not absent. We may not understand His silence when it is part of a redirection notice. Context and time will show it, but in the meantime, it is no less real. From our perspective, a certain route may not make sense. But I recall that Ravi Zacharias once stated something to the effect that, "When our limited understanding does not line up with God's infinite wisdom, we must accept that His ways are not our ways".[41] He is sovereign. We must accept that there may be things that we are not aware of. I have accepted that at the right time, action will happen and healing will occur. But until then, I would like to think that my ability to stop and listen for God's voice has improved over time, and I have found that He has always been faithful, so I can trust Him.

When the door closes, I have learned to watch out for when God opens a window. And when it comes along, I have the confidence to jump through it. So, my current aim nowadays is to be listening and jump when the window is presented and glorify Him. I know that it may not necessarily be welcome at the time, but I have found that if our eyes stay focused on Him, we come out the other side of hardship better for it. When we are in the situation, we may not be able to see how an end could possibly come. But I assure you, it will. Even if this is only as we learn to cope with and accept the situation, and we may be holding tightly onto His leg to help us stand, just as a toddler will cling tightly to a parent's leg while they learn to walk.

Yes, I have lost physical ability, but this has helped me to appreciate those things that I still have. I may not know what is around the corner tomorrow, but I know Him who holds every tomorrow in His hands, having them all planned out for me. Just because I may not understand why I am on the path that I have been put and am still on does not mean that He is not leading me. As He promises in Isaiah 42:16b, "I will lead them in paths they have not known. I will make darkness light before them, and crooked places straight. These things I will do for them, and not forsake them."

We cannot dictate to God where and how He is to move. Do not tell God that He has to act according to your time frame. He often will not act according to our expectations. He is God; we are not. His ways are not our ways. When He does not act as we would prefer, we need to look to see what lessons He wants us to learn or wait to see what He will do. If there is a delay, we can be sure that there is something we are not privy to. But regardless, our (my) place is to bring Him glory in whatever circumstance we find ourselves.

A book by Brennan Manning titled *The Ragamuffin Gospel*[42] touches on the concept of receiving a second calling while being rebuilt in solitude and receiving understanding while on a quest for His presence. At this point, I too have a stronger desire for intimacy with God and renewal than for healing. It is almost as if, yes, healing will come, but first there are some other things, including becoming more Christlike, that are higher on my to-do list in life.

Whether healing comes or not, my prayer is that I will be used in whatever state I may be in, frailty and all, to bring glory to God, where it belongs.

He has told me, "You Are Mine". He is faithful, so in His sovereignty, I can trust Him because everything that happens to me can be used for His glory. I may have MS, but I can say that if this is to be the extent of my suffering, then I am quite happy to suffer for Him, and I know that whatever else comes my way, He has allowed me to go through it. I will not complain if it means that I can bring Him glory! It is all good.

If we keep our eyes fixed on Jesus, He will direct our steps along the path that is best for us. And no matter what we go through here in this life (in my case, healed or unhealed), we can look forward to life beyond either the grave or Christ's return (whichever comes first), where everything will be made new if we are His. This became very real to me in the midst of disability. He has been faithful in all areas of life—study, family, relationships, and children to name just a few. I have found that He is a God who is present and faithful even when things do not make sense. I now have ultimate contentment.

My life was pulled apart and rebuilt. I have sought healing, but as yet, it has not come. One day, however, I know it will eventually come (maybe even once my race here on earth ends and I receive an ultimate upgrade). And finally, there are just four thoughts left to share:

- I am confined to a wheelchair, but it is all good because "You Are Mine".
- I have MS, and it may get worse, but it is all good because He is faithful.
- I may not know the how's or why's, but it is all good because He is sovereign.
- My identity and self-confidence do not lie in health and well-being; they lie in Christ in whom I can trust.

So, it is *all good!*

Postscript

After having read this book, I want to make one thing abundantly clear. I am *not* a spiritual giant like William Carey, DL Moody, Corrie ten Boone, Doris van Stone, or many others. I am on this journey with ups and downs, just like anyone else. I wish it was all up, but it is not. I wish I could have each of their testimonies, but I cannot because God has taken me along a different path. Please understand that this book is about His faithfulness (not anything about me). So, if anything seems way up there out of reach in the stratosphere of Christian maturity, it is not what I want to convey. It was and is all down to Him.

When I was younger, I would read biographies of Christian ground breakers such as those mentioned above, and I would feel discouraged, inadequate, unprepared, and generally a failure in my own Christian walk. I do not claim to be among any Christian legends. I am just a traveler on the journey along with many others. None of us are perfect, just forgiven, as these legends would testify. And that is what is important—not how perfectly we walk but that we walk at all. We should, however, aim to always walk closer to Christ with less stumbling. My advice is to always, always run the race so that one day you will hear, "Well done, good and faithful servant" (Mat 25:21). This book is about God's faithfulness. Now—go out, 'walk the walk, run the race' (see 2 Tim 4:7), bring Him glory, and be faithful!

What Next?

To make things 'All Good'.

Having read this book, you may have the thought, *It is wonderful that he feels that it is all good even though he has something as bad as MS. Good for him! If only I could say that too.*

Let me share with you some good news.

Jesus Christ lived for one purpose alone: to die for you. The relationship with God was broken by Adam and Eve long ago. And the only way this relationship could be restored was by payment of shed blood (originally done by animal sacrifice). But this payment was only temporary, not perfect. Sin was impregnated through everyone. It needed someone perfect to shed blood. So God sent His own son to die for us some two thousand years ago. If we accept this free gift, that relationship will be restored and everything will be all good again.

It does not mean that we will avoid hardships (like MS), the most important thing is what comes after this life. It is eternity (and eternity is much longer!). If things are all good, you will spend eternity with God. If not, you will not. You choose   go with God or Satan. Heaven or hell.

In the words of a song I once heard, "I am going to heaven. Would you like to come along too?" If you would like to make things right, and accept that gift, you can pray this prayer:

> Dear God,
> I know that I am a sinner and need You.
> I believe Jesus Christ was Your son and that He died for my sins and then rose again.
> Thank you for the free gift that You offer—forgiveness and life everlasting.
> I accept it and make You number one in my life, asking You to be my Lord—not just Savior but Lord and King as well.

Please send Your Holy Spirit to show and teach me how
to live.
Thank you that we have a restored relationship.
In Jesus's name,
Amen.

If you prayed this prayer, welcome to the family of God. Find a Bible-believing church, share it with someone, and start the most exciting journey you will ever embark on—down the road of life with God.

Now, I would make two suggestions. Your salvation doesn't depend on them but to grow in Christian maturity – they *will* help!

Firstly – Go to a fellow believer and let them know about your decision. It is important to own both your decision and Christ. Eventually, you will have to stand in front of those who will be antagonistic. And what better way to start, than by standing up in front of those who love you. They can encourage and spur you on in your new journey.

Secondly – Find a Bible-believing church and get involved. You can't do this journey on your own! That's why the writer to the Hebrews implored them not to give up meeting together in Hebrews 10:25. I think of people I knew in the past who said, "I'll do it on my own, Thank You!" They have fallen right away now.

Appendix 1

Rushing Wind (Green/Green 1977)[43]

Rushing wind blow through this temple,
Blowing out the dust within,
Come and breathe your breath upon me,
I've been born again.

Holy spirit, I surrender,
Take me where you want to go,
Plant me by your living water,
Plant me deep so I can grow.

Jesus, you're the one, who sets my spirit free,
Use me lord, glorify, your holy name through me.
Separate me from this world lord.
Sanctify my life for you.
Daily change me to your image,
Help me bear good fruit.
Every day you're drawing closer.

Trials come to test my faith.
But when all is said and done lord,
You know, it was worth the wait.
Jesus, you're the one, who set my spirit free,
Use me lord, glorify, your holy name through me.

Rushing wind blow through this temple,
Blowing out the dust within,
Come and breathe your breath upon me,
For I've been born again.

Appendix 2

I Sit, I Stand (Mark Elvery 1996)

In the quiet of the midnight hour,
I sit on the shore listening.
The wind gently blows in off the lake
To bring waves that lap the shore.
Above, clouds blow in from the ocean
To partly obscure the moon and stars.
Yet in the breaks,
I see the blazing Southern Cross,
Undisturbed by clouds far below
Who try to mask its glory.
And though it may be
Hidden from sight for a time,
It is still there in all its splendor and glory,
The ultimate marker in the southern sky.
Across the lake, far off,
An undulating bright light reaches me,
As if God is watching me from afar,
As if He has hidden His face.
But I know that though His presence
May be obscured from sight
By heavy clouds of hardship and despair,
He is always there, feeling what I feel,
Lapping at my soul's door to assure
With the words, "My grace is all you need."
I stand to look out over God's creation,
Sensing how He felt on that night.
The wind in my face,
I pray the Lord, His Spirit, to blow on me
Vigor and understanding,
To know my awesome God.

Come, Holy Spirit.
Come blow over this broken life,
For God has given, and He has taken away.
But I will never lose my eternal inheritance,
So why are you downcast, O my soul?
The things of earth will pass
And grow strangely dim,
But the Word of the Lord
Will burn—an unquenchable fire.
Lord, immerse me in your decrees,
That I may live in them
Both now and forevermore.

Amen

Appendix 3

I Stand in Awe (Mark Elvery 1996)

I stand in awe of Your creation.
The handiwork of Your great love
Above, clouds as majestic
As anything in the sky,
More variant than the birds of the air,
Bringing life-giving water
To the parched soil of this land.
In the same way, You bring
Sustaining and refreshing words
To this, the parched soil of my soul.
Oh, my heart longs
For the knowledge of You,
That I may find favor in Your eyes
So that You may smile upon me.
Behind me, cliffs of sand
Rise from the earth!
Many their colors.
They stand by You alone, O God!
You created the earth
Before You walked it as a man.
You planned every color
And in time formed every grain of sand.
You knew its shape, content,
And every movement it would make
Upon the chaotic wind and wave.
So much more
Do you know my life and being!
Nothing surprises You;
No—*Nothing!!*
May You teach me Your word

That I may ever walk in it.
Before me, the churning sea.
White water surges
As waves crash down.
Oh, to be submerged
Within that chaotic water,
Being pulled under, twisted, and turned,
Unable to catch your breath
As you slowly sink beneath its fury.
Oh, how the wicked one desires
To throw chaos into Your plans, O God.
Do not let me sink
In waves of terror and the unknown.
Lift me up to higher ground
That I may worship You
All the days of my life.
To the author of all creation and knowledge.
You alone are the Almighty.
To the God of power and justice,
You are Adonai.
To the King of kings and Lord of lords,
You are the great I Am.
To Jehovah Jireh, El Shaddai,
You know and supply my every need.
To the God who stooped down
To save a wretch like me,
You are my Redeemer, Emmanuel.
But of all these great and glorious names,
You are my God and my Father.

Amen

Appendix 4

Take Hold (Mark Elvery 1994)

(Verse 1)   No matter where you come from,
Or where you're goin' to,
Jesus Christ was crucified
And still is lovin' you.
You can't run or hide from Him.
There's nothing you can do.

(Chorus)   Take hold, Take hold,
Take hold, my friend.
Take hold, This moment.
Could be your last chance.
Yesterday is gone;
Tomorrow may not come.
So, Take hold, Take hold,
Take hold, my friend,
Of this moment now.

(Verse 2)   No matter what your experience
Or pressures you may feel,
There is a friend who loves you.
His strength, yours when you kneel.
You can lean on him no matter what,
A friend so true and real. (So...)

(Chorus)

(Verse 3)   Whether in times of laughter
Or times when you may bleed,
There is One who shares it all.
He's in our holy creed,
Comforter and Prince of Peace,
The Son of God is He.

(Bridge)   Take hold, come now
(It's) your moment now! (x 2)

(Verse 4)   No higher, no wider,
You'll find forgiveness is
Nothing more and nothing less.
It's all you'll ever need.
No longer run and hide.
Just fall in his open arms (and …)

(Chorus x2)

Notes

1   Green/Green, "Rushing Wind"
2   Green/Hazard, "No Compromise – The Life Story of Keith Green"
3   Green/Green, "Rushing Wind"
4   Tada, interview between Joni Eareckson Tada and Pastor Greg Laurie, 2016.
5   Ibid.
6   Watts, 1674-1748.
7   Keller, *Walking with God through Pain and Suffering* (London: Hodder & Stoughton, 2016).
8   Tada, interview between Joni Eareckson Tada and Pastor Greg Laurie, 2016.
9   van Stone, *Dorie: The Girl Nobody Loved* (Chicago: The Moody Bible Institute, 1981) p. 151
10 Swindoll, *David – A Man of Passion and Destiny* (Nashville: W Publishing Group, 1997) p. 73
11 van Stone, *Dorie: The Girl Nobody Loved* (Chicago: The Moody Bible Institute, 1981) p. 69-71
12 Ibid. p. 73
13 Ibid. p. 70-72
14 Green, "Run To the End the Highway"
15 van Stone, *Dorie: The Girl Nobody Loved* (Chicago: The Moody Bible Institute, 1981) p. 150
16 Green, "Run To the End the Highway"
17 van Stone, *Dorie: The Girl Nobody Loved* (Chicago: The Moody Bible Institute, 1981) p. 79-80
18 Ibid. p. 141
19 Ibid. p. 74
20 Marks, "Single-Minded Love"
21 Casting Crowns, "Praise You In This Storm"
22 Redman, "Blessed Be Your Name"
23 Chapman, "God is God"
24 Tada, "Hope: The Best of Things." 2005.
25 Grubb, *Rees Howells – Intercessor* (Cambridge: The Lutterworth Press, 1952)
26 Roever, *From Tragedy to Triumph*. Roever and Associates, 1988 (Updated 2009).
27 Roever, *Scarred* (Fort Worth: Roever Communications, 1995)
28 Chapman, "That's Paradise"

29   Elvery, Mark W. *"Congratulations, You Have MS."* Luke's Journal (CMDFA) 18, no. 1 (April 2013):p. 10-11.

30   Hamblin, "This 'Ole House"

31   Tada, "National Religious Broadcasters Convention Address." 2013

32   Owen, Public Testimony before the Subcommittee on Labor, Health and Human Services and Education, Senate Subcomitee on Appropriations. 2000, 0:57:29-1:07:49.

33   Chapman, "That's Paradise"

34   Iversen, "Spirit of the Living God"

35   Keller, *Walking with God through Pain and Suffering* (London: Hodder & Stoughton, 2016)

36   Owen, Public Testimony before the Subcommittee on Labor, Health and Human Services and Education, Senate Subcomitee on Appropriations. 2000, 0:57:29-1:07:49.

37   Ibid. 2000

38   Ibid. 2000

39   Tada, "Interview between Joni Eareckson Tada and Charles Swindoll at Stonebriar Community Church." 2015.

40   Ibid. 2015

41   Zacharias, "Let My People Think." Heard on 87.8 FM.

42   Manning, *The Ragamuffin Gospel* (Colorado Springs: Multnomah Books, 1990)

43   Green/Green, "Rushing Wind"

Bibliography

Bible Translations

- Holy Bible, New International Version, NIV®. Copyright ©1973, 1978, 1984, 2011 by Biblica, Inc.™ Used by permission of Zondervan. All rights reserved worldwide.
  www.zondervan.com
- New Revised Standard Version Bible, copyright ©1989 by National Council of the Churches of Christ in the United States of America. Used by permission. All rights reserved worldwide.
- King James Version—public domain.

Citations

Casting Crowns "Praise You In This Storm" on Lifesong. Mark A. Miller. © 2005 Word Music LLC. Compact disc.

Chapman, Stephen Curtis "That's Paradise" on The Great Adventure. Phil Naish. © 1992 BMG Chrysalis. Cassette.

Chapman, Stephen Curtis "God is God" on Declaration. Brown Banner & Stephen Curtis Chapman. © 2001 BMG Chrysalis. Electronic.

Elvery, Mark W. "Congratulations, You Have MS." Luke's Journal (CMDFA) 18, no. 1 (April 2013): 10-11. Used by permission.

Green, Keith "Run to the End the Highway" on Jesus Commands Us to Go! Bill Maxwell. © 1984 Sparrow. Vinyl recording.

Green, Melody and Green, Keith "Rushing Wind" on No Compromise. Bill Maxwell. © 1977 EMI April Music Inc. for Australia and New Zealand: EMI Music Publishing Australia Pty Limited (ABN 83 000 040 951) Locked Bag 7300, Darlinghurst NSW 1300. Australia International copyright securing. All rights reserved. Vinyl recording. Used by permission.

Green, Melody and Hazard, David "No Compromise – The Life Story of Keith Green" (Nashville, Thomas Nelson, 1989)

Grubb, Norman P., "Rees Howells – Intercessor" (Cambridge: The Lutterworth Press, 1952)

Hamblin, Stuart. "This 'Ole House", © 1954.

Iversen, Daniel "Spirit of the Living God", © 1935.

Keller, Tim, "Walking With God Through Pain And Suffering" (London: Hodder & Stoughton, 2016), Kindle location 2684-2688, 2834-2835

Manning, Brennan "The Ragamuffin Gospel" (Colorado Springs: Multnomah Books, 1990)

Marks, Kenny "Single-Minded Love" on Right Where You Are. Keith Thomas. © 1984 Word Inc. Vinyl recording. Used by permission.

Owen, Mary Jane "Public Testimony before the Subcommittee on Labor, Health and Human Services and Education, Senate Subcommittee on Appropriations" Cong., 0:57:29-1:07:49 (2000). URL: https://www.c-span.org/video/?156796-1/stem-cell-research Accessed 7/11/2017

Redman, Matt "Blessed Be Your Name" on Where Angels Fear to Tread. Dwayne Laming & Jason Halbert. © 2002 ThankYou Music. Compact disc.

Roever, Dave, "From Tragedy to Triumph". Roever and Associates, © 1988 (Updated 2009). VHS.

Roever, Dave, "Scarred" (Fort Worth: Roever Communications, 1995). VHS

Swindoll, Charles R. "David – A Man of Passion and Destiny" (Nashville: W Publishing Group, © 1997) Used by permission, 73

Tada, Joni Eareckson "Hope: The Best of Things". Address. 2005. Accessed January 21, 2018. https://www.desiringgod.org/messages/suffering-for-the-sake-of. Used with Permission

Tada, Joni Eareckson "Interview between Joni Eareckson Tada and Charles Swindoll" Interview By Charles Swindoll at Stonebriar Community Church. YouTube. June 17, 2015. Accessed November 7, 2017. Https://www.Youtube.com/Watch?V=8CGdWg7HWT4. Used by permission

Tada, Joni Eareckson "National Religious Broadcasters Convention Address." Address. 2013. Accessed November 7, 2017. www.youtube.com/watch?v=jrO5fGSIyM8. Used by permission

Tada, Joni Eareckson "Harvest – Greg Laurie Interview with Joni Eareckson Tada." Interview by Greg Laurie. YouTube. 2016. Accessed November 7, 2017. https://www.youtube.com/watch?v=iK19MsJVsdY. Used by permission from Harvest Ministries with Greg Laurie, PO Box 4000, Riverside, CA 92514 van Stone, Doris "Dorie: The Girl Nobody Loved" (Chicago: The Moody Bible Institute, © 1981) Used by permission of Moody Publishers, 14; 69-71; 70-72; 73; 74; 79-80; 150; 151

Watts, Isaac n.d. Accessed November 7, 2017. www.google.com.au

Zacharias, Ravi "Let My People Think" 97.8 FM. www.rzim.org All rights reserved. Used with permission.

Other Recommendations and References

Ruscoe, Dorothy. "The Intercession of Rees Howells". (Cambridge: The Lutterworth Press, © 1983, 1988, 1991, 2003, 2011)

Tada, Joni Eareckson "Interview between Joni Eareckson Tada and Greg Laurie. Joni shares a Lifetime of Wisdom" A New Beginning. As heard on Vision Radio 97.6 FM, 5 April 2016.

Tada, Joni Eareckson "A Place of Healing, wrestling with the mysteries of suffering, pain and God's sovereignty" (Colorado Springs: David C Cook © 2010)

- "Reading Mark's journey with MS from those early symptoms till his present condition revealed an honest encounter with the living God that expressed the transformative power of grace. Despite the challenges of broken relationships, at many levels God has proved sufficient along the way whether that is in distress and isolation or the joy of God's provision when it seemed impossible. It is a confronting, honest and inspiring journey of faith."

    Jeff Ireland – *Senior Pastor, Wynnum Baptist Church. Brisbane, Qld, Australia.*

- "Everyone of us will encounter challenges in life. Few of us will encounter what author Mark Elvery has encountered.

    This cogent, thoughtful, and compelling book speaks to the enormous power of faith, grace and mercy in the face of struggle. His life is a testimony to God's gentle guiding hands in the darkest moments imaginable.

    I Cor 13:12 is proven to be true in Mark's life: 'For now, I see through a glass darkly, but one day, I will see as I am seen, face-to-face. One day I will know, as I am known. Until that day, 3 things remain: FAITH, HOPE, and LOVE, and the greatest of these is LOVE'.

    I found the telling of his story to be riveting & honest, while constantly seeing & reminding us how our steps in life have meaning & have been ordered by a loving Savior.

    Moving from the earthshaking diagnosis of MS, pursuit of a career in dentistry, falling in love, marriage and the hope of having children, Mark sees it all with profound maturity.

    He is a skillful author and, using the powerful word 'CONGRATULATIONS', (as you'll read in the opening chapter), we can be deeply encouraged in whatever difficulties come our way. Read this book and share its insights with everyone you know… CONGRATULATIONS!"

    Kenny Marks – *Singer, Songwriter, Recording Artist and fellow believer on life's journey. Nashville, TN, USA.*

A week after this endorsement was received,
Kenny died following a heart attack
– the end of his journey in this life. He was 67.
6.11.1950 – 31.10.2018

- "In this heart warming and yet challenging book, Mark opens up in honest and sometimes confronting ways about his journey with MS. Yet, while his book exposes the extreme challenges of living with the progressively debilitating effects of the disease, his book is not so much a story about the physical and emotional strain of living with MS but rather it is the story of his journey with Jesus in the midst of it all. In this journey Mark has discovered that there is a healing that God offers in the here-and-now which is even greater than the immediate healing of our bodies. It is the healing of our souls!

  With profound personal and theological insights, discovered in God's Word and in the crucible of adversity, Mark helps us all see that, no matter our physical condition, we all face disability of one kind or another because we have all experienced the ravages of sin and defeat. And the only real answer for each one of us is to be found in a deep, personal relationship of faith and trust in Jesus Christ who alone has the power to save us and ultimately make all things new.

  Peter Francis – *Principal of Malyon Theological College. Qld, Australia.*

- "The point is – God is faithful; therefore, ALL things work together for good. You know how hard life can be, but do you also know how faithful God is? This is a story of not just the reality of life, but the reality of God's faithfulness as He rebuilds a broken life. An encouraging yet confronting change to much literature today."

  Dave Roever – *International speaker, decorated Vietnam veteran. Fort Worth, TX, USA.*

- This quote from the book sums up the remarkable life of Mark Elvery, "There is no event in one's life that is pointless or useless when that life is handed over to God". The content is biblically based, and tells Mark's inspirational story about finding the Lord in each moment of our lives, including the dark times. We can all relate to the fight to accept the overwhelming and undeserved grace of Christ.

  Linda Nevell – *Editor of the QB Magazine. Qld, Australia.*

Printed in the United States
By Bookmasters